VOLUME 10

THE NEW GLOBAL ERA

THE ILLUSTRATED
HISTORY OF THE WORLD

VOLUME 10
THE NEW GLOBAL ERA

J. M. ROBERTS

DUNCAN BAIRD PUBLISHERS

LONDON

The Illustrated History of the World

This edition first published in Great Britain in 1999

Duncan Baird Publishers
Sixth Floor
Castle House
75–76 Wells Street
London W1P 3RE

THE NEW GLOBAL ERA
Copyright © Editorial Debate SA 1998
Text Copyright © J. M. Roberts 1976, 1980, 1983, 1987, 1988, 1992, 1998
Artwork and Diagrams Copyright © Editorial Debate SA 1998
(for copyright of photographs, maps and diagrams, see acknowledgments on page 192,
which are to be regarded as an extension of this copyright)

Art Direction by Duncan Baird Publishers
Produced by Duncan Baird Publishers, London, England,
and Editorial Debate, Madrid, Spain

British Library Cataloguing-in-Publication Data:
A catalogue record for this book is available from the British Library.

ISBN 1-900131-73-0

DBP team:
Senior editor: Joanne Levêque
Assistant editors: Georgina Harris, Kirsty Seymour-Ure
Senior designer: Steven Painter
Assistant designer: Anita Schnable
Picture research: Julia Ruxton
Sales fulfilment: Ian Smalley
Map artwork: Russell Bell
Decorative borders: Lorraine Harrison

Editorial Debate team:
Editors and picture researchers:
Isabel Belmonte Martínez, Feliciano Novoa Portela,
Ruth Betegón Díez, Dolores Redondo
Editorial coordination: Ana Lucía Vila

Typeset in Sabon 11/15 pt
Colour reproduction by Trescan, Madrid, Spain
Printed in Singapore by Imago Limited

NOTE
The abbreviations CE and BCE are used throughout this book:
CE Common Era (the equivalent of AD)
BCE Before Common Era (the equivalent of BC)

10 9 8 7 6 5 4 3 2 1

CONTENTS

THE NEW GLOBAL ERA

THE CONTINUING ACCELERATION of historical change which has characterized the last five hundred years or so has been more striking than ever since 1945. For some peoples and societies, the pace of change has literally been intolerable. We live in a world still unsettled by the global revolution in economic and political organization which began during the Second World War and has been going on ever since. Two and a half decades during which the central characteristics of the world political order seemed to be more and more frozen (though revolutionary developments were continuing elsewhere) were to be followed by a renewed quickening of the pace of change in the 1980s. By the end of that decade, landmarks taken for granted for thirty years and more had disappeared (sometimes almost overnight) and others, even more dominating, were already called in question. The whole process was so rapid and continuous as to make divisions in the story unusually artificial, but the historian has to try to analyse and uncover their structure. Some of the forces behind the turmoil were very profound and very mixed. Some, for instance, were rooted in the growing energy needs of industrialized societies already touched upon. Others can be traced ultimately much further back – to, for example, ideas first announced in the French Revolution. But though it is worth striving for as deep a historical perspective as possible, the long-term trends and forces cannot alone explain what happened. Like other great changes throughout history, many of those of the second half of the twentieth century arose almost from accident, circumstance, even personality. They are none the easier to explain for that.

Since 1985, Europe has undergone extraordinary changes much more quickly than most people ever imagined possible. The "Iron Curtain" that once divided Western and Eastern Europe disappeared in the space of a few short years, giving rise to numerous political, economic, psychological and military disturbances. With the era of perestroika (restructuring) and glasnost (openness) in the Soviet Union and the fall of the Berlin Wall, political and economic objectives, as well as international relations, were redefined in Eastern Europe. Here, East Berliners watch a section of the wall being torn down in late 1989. Many people kept pieces of it as a souvenir of the "wall of shame".

1 THE POLITICS OF THE NEW WORLD

IN THE DECADES following the end of the Second World War, world history was dominated by a prolonged and bitter Soviet–American antagonism. The "Cold War" made the rupture in the diplomatic history of the modern era which had first opened in 1917 the dominating fact of world affairs. The future great power which made its appearance through the Bolshevik coup was to approach international society in a new and uniquely troublesome way. Soviet Russia regarded diplomacy not just as a convenient way of doing business but as a weapon for the

advance of ideology. However they qualified it in practice, Bolsheviks had said their aim was to overthrow the social institutions of non-communist societies, and they meant it, so far as the long run was concerned. After 1945 other communist states came into existence whose rulers agreed, at least in words. The result was a world seemingly divided into two camps, one led by the USSR, one by the United States. Each camp proclaimed itself as anti-imperialist. Each often, in fact, behaved (if effective domination is the test) in imperialist ways.

Wilhelm Pieck (1876–1960) is pictured here being congratulated on the day he was elected president of the German Democratic Republic in 1949. East Germany was eventually to emerge as the leading satellite state in the East European bloc.

GERMANY DIVIDED

THE ORIGINAL COMMUNIST Europe of 1945 had been added to by other takeovers in 1947 as Hungary, Romania and Poland ceased to have any non-Communists in their governments. Czechoslovakia followed in 1948. Then, the opening of the Marshall Aid programme was almost at once followed by what was to prove to be the first battle of the Cold War, over the fate of Berlin. It was decisive. It established the point at which, in Europe, the United States was prepared to fight. It does not seem that this outcome had been anticipated by the Russians, though they had provoked it by seeking to prevent the re-emergence of a reunited and economically powerful Germany which would not be under their control. The Western powers had a different interest, to reanimate the German economy, at the very least in their own occupation zones. They sought to get on with this before Germany's future political shape was settled, sure that it was vital for the recovery of Western Europe as a whole.

In 1948, without Russian agreement, the Western powers introduced a currency reform in their own sectors. It had a galvanic effect, releasing the process of economic recovery in western Germany. Following on Marshall Aid, available (thanks to Soviet decisions) only to the Western-occupied zones, this reform, more than any other step, cut Germany in two. It meant that the recovery of the eastern half would not be integrated with that of Western Europe. A strong western

Germany might now emerge by itself. That the Western powers should get on with the business of putting German industry on its feet was undoubtedly economic sense, but eastern Germany was thenceforth decisively on the other side of the Iron Curtain. Currency reform divided Berlin, too, and thereby prejudiced Communist chances of staging a popular putsch in the city.

West Berlin police greet Berliners returning to their sector of the city in 1953.

Time chart (1948–1974)

	1948 Berlin crisis and air shuttle	1952 Nasser becomes president of Egypt	1959 Castro imposes a Communist régime in Cuba	1967 The Arab–Israeli Six Day War	
1940			1960		1980
	1950 Start of the Korean War	1955 Bandung Conference	1962 Missile crisis in Cuba	1964 Start of the Vietnam War	1974 The "Revolution of the Carnations" in Portugal

An American aeroplane carrying food supplies arrives in West Berlin. Throughout the blockade, the British and Americans ran an air shuttle, with a plane taking off or landing every minute, to ferry supplies to the city.

THE BERLIN AIRLIFT

The Soviet response to the Western powers' introduction of currency reform was to disrupt communication between the Western zones of Germany and Berlin. Whatever their original motives, the dispute escalated. Some Western officials had already had it in mind that a severance of Western Berlin from the three Western occupation zones (Berlin was isolated inside the Soviet zone) might be attempted before this crisis; the word "blockade" had been used and the Russians' acts were now interpreted in this sense. They had not interfered with the rights of the Western allies to have access to their own forces in their own sectors of Berlin, but they were interfering with the traffic which ensured supply to the Berliners in those sectors. To supply West Berlin, the British and Americans organized an airlift to the city. The Russians wanted to demonstrate to the West Berliners that the Western powers could not stay there if they did not want them to; they hoped thus to remove the obstacle which the presence of elected non-Communist municipal authorities presented to Soviet control of Berlin. The Western powers, in spite of the enormous cost of maintaining such a flow of food, fuel and medicine as would just keep West Berlin going, announced they were prepared to keep it up indefinitely. The implication was that they could be stopped only by force. For the first time since the war American strategic bombers moved back to bases in England. Neither side wanted to fight, but all hope of cooperation over Germany on the basis of wartime agreement was dead.

THE FOUNDATION OF NATO

The blockade of West Berlin lasted over a year and defeating it was a remarkable technical achievement. Berlin's only airfield had to handle over a thousand aircraft a day for most of the time, with an average daily delivery of 5,000 tons of coal alone. Yet its real significance was political. Allied supply was not interrupted nor were the West Berliners intimidated. The Soviet authorities made the best of defeat by deliberately splitting the city and refusing the mayor access to his office. Meanwhile the Western powers had signed a treaty setting up a new alliance, the North Atlantic Treaty Organization (NATO), in April 1949, a few weeks before the blockade was ended by agreement. NATO was the first Cold War creation to transcend Europe. The United States and Canada were members, as well as most Western European states (only Sweden, Switzerland and Spain did not join). It was explicitly a defensive alliance, providing for the mutual defence of any member attacked and so yet another break with the now almost-vanished isolationist traditions of American foreign policy. In May a new German state, the Federal Republic, emerged from the three western zones of occupation and in the following October, a German Democratic Republic (the GDR) was set up in the east. Henceforth, there were to be two Germanies, it seemed, and the Cold War ran along an Iron Curtain dividing them, and not, as Churchill had suggested in 1946, further east, from Trieste to Stettin. But a particularly dangerous phase in Europe was over.

The West German chancellor, Konrad Adenauer (1876–1967) (middle row, second from left), is among the members of the Council of Ministers attending this NATO Council meeting in 1955. It was during this meeting, when West Germany was formally admitted, that the North Atlantic Treaty Organization acquired its full significance as a defence against Communism.

North Atlantic Treaty 1949

"The Parties agree that an armed attack on one or more of them in Europe or North America shall be considered an attack against them all and they consequently agree that, if such an armed attack occurs, each of them, in exercise of the right of individual or collective self-defence recognized by Article 51 of the Charter of the United Nations, will assist the Party or Parties so attacked by taking forthwith, individually in concert with the other Parties, such action as it deems necessary, including the use of armed force, to restore and maintain the security of the North Atlantic area. Any such armed attack and all measures taken as a result thereof shall immediately be reported to the Security Council. Such measures shall be terminated when the Security Council has taken the measures necessary to restore and maintain international peace and security."

An extract from Article 5 of the North Atlantic Treaty of 1949.

The Cold War

The Second World War had given rise to an alliance between countries of very different political tendencies. However, this alliance disappeared once the war was over. Although the United States and the Soviet Union were not to engage in direct conflict, their rivalry from 1945 onwards turned into a confrontation known as the Cold War, a term coined by a journalist reporting on an unfruitful meeting to control nuclear energy in 1946.

In 1947 disagreements between the superpowers came to the fore when the Soviet leaders rejected the Americans' Marshall Plan. Instead, the USSR created COMECON in 1949 and installed Soviet systems in the Eastern bloc.

During the long period of the Cold War, four main stages could be discerned. Each stage began with rising tensions, followed by a breakdown in relations, generally with a regional war, but eventually ending in more cordial relations. In the first stage (1945–1953), both blocs took up irreconcilable positions and there was no dialogue at all between them. This stage culminated in the Korean War. Between 1953 and 1962, after Stalin's death, Khrushchev began talks, first with Eisenhower and then with Kennedy. The impact of the Cuban Missile Crisis in 1962 forced both sides to consider the dangers of a nuclear war. During the third stage (1962–1973), overshadowed by the Vietnam War, the two military superpowers proposed limiting the acquisition of strategic weapons, which were ruining their economies. Between 1973 and 1989, attention was first focused on the world economic crisis, but the war in Afghanistan muddied the waters of their relations again. This phase differs from earlier ones in that East–West conflicts were stabilized, while North–South conflicts came to the fore. In 1989, the world view changed totally with the withdrawal of the Soviet troops from Afghanistan, Gorbachev's proposal for disarmament and the democratic changes in Eastern Europe.

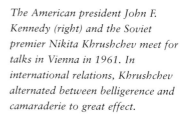

The American president John F. Kennedy (right) and the Soviet premier Nikita Khrushchev meet for talks in Vienna in 1961. In international relations, Khrushchev alternated between belligerence and camaraderie to great effect.

THE KOREAN WAR

The foundation of NATO suggested perhaps that as well as two Europes, there might also be two worlds. This soon seemed more likely still, when the Cold War re-erupted in East Asia. In 1945 Korea had been divided along the 38th parallel, its industrial north being occupied by the Russians and the agricultural south by the Americans. The problem of reunification was eventually referred to the United Nations. After efforts to obtain elections for the whole country that organization recognized a government set up in the south as the only lawful government of the Republic of Korea. By then, the Soviet zone also had a government claiming sovereignty over the whole country. After Russian and American forces had both withdrawn, North Korean forces invaded the south in June 1950 (with, it now appears, Stalin's foreknowledge and approval). Within two days President Truman sent American forces to fight them, acting in the name of the United Nations. The Security Council had voted to resist aggression, and as the Russians were at that moment boycotting it, they could not veto United Nations action.

The Americans always provided the bulk of the UN forces in Korea, but other nations soon sent contingents. Within a few months the allied army was operating well north of the 38th parallel. It seemed likely that the North Koreans would be overthrown. When fighting drew near the Manchurian border, though, Chinese Communist forces intervened and drove back the UN army. There was now a danger of a much bigger conflict. The question arose of direct action, possibly with nuclear weapons, by the United States against China. China was the second largest Communist state in the world, and the largest in terms of population. Behind it stood the USSR; a man could walk from Erfurt in East Germany to Shanghai without once leaving Communist territory.

Prudently, Truman insisted that the United States must not become involved in a greater war on the Asian mainland. That much settled, further fighting showed that although the Chinese might be able to keep the North Koreans in the field, they could not overturn South Korea against American wishes. Armistice talks were started. The new

The Korean War

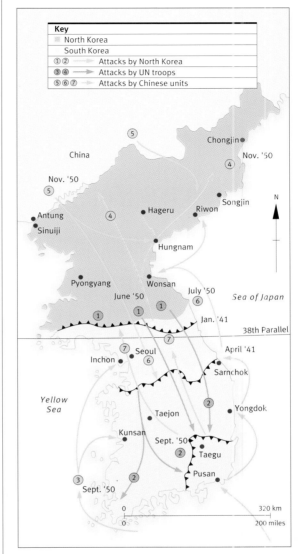

In 1950, the conflict in Korea became the first in which the risk of a nuclear war between the superpowers was apparent. Until then, diplomatic crises and local wars had created varying degrees of tension between East and West. The danger of another world war, however, had been remote, as the United States had a monopoly on atomic warheads. But when the Soviet Union successfully carried out its first atomic test in August 1949, the world realized that a nuclear holocaust was possible. Fears mounted when the two superpowers entered into conflict over Korea, even though they were not directly at war with each other, as the map shows.

The main strategic events of the Korean War are depicted.

American administration which came into office in 1953 was Republican and unequivocally anti-Communist, but knew its predecessor had sufficiently demonstrated its will and capacity to uphold an independent South Korea and felt that the real centre of the Cold War was in Europe rather than in Asia. The armistice was signed in July 1953. Subsequent efforts to turn this into a formal peace have as yet failed; almost half a century later, tension remains high between the two Koreas.

In the Far East as well as in Europe the Americans had won the first battles of the Cold War, and in Korea they had been real battles; estimates suggest the war cost three million casualties in all, civilians included.

THE USSR AT STALIN'S DEATH

SHORTLY BEFORE THE ARMISTICE that ended the Korean War in 1953, Stalin had died. It was very difficult to guess what this might mean. In due course, there seemed to have been something of a break in the continuity of Soviet policy, but that was not clear at the time. The American president Eisenhower remained distrustful of Russian intentions and in the middle of the 1950s, the Cold War was as intense as ever. Shortly after Stalin's death his successors revealed that they too had the improved nuclear weapon known as the hydrogen bomb. It was in a way Stalin's final memorial. It guaranteed (if it had been in doubt) the USSR's status in the post-war world. Stalin had carried to their logical conclusion the repressive policies of Lenin, but he had done much more than his predecessor. He had rebuilt most of the tsarist empire and had given Russia the strength to survive (just, and with the help of powerful allies) her gravest hour of trial. What is not clear is that this could only have been achieved or was worth achieving at such cost, unless (as may well be thought) to have escaped German domination was justification enough. The Soviet Union was a great power, but, among the elements of that empire, Russia at least would doubtless have become one again without communism, and her peoples had been rewarded for their sufferings with precious little but an assurance of international strength. Domestic life after the war was harsher than ever; consumption was for years still held down and both the propaganda to which Soviet citizens were subjected and the brutalities of the police system seemed, if anything, to have been intensified after some relaxation during the war.

A Soviet propaganda poster from 1950 shows Stalin advocating "the Leninist path to communism". The dam in the background is meant to illustrate the Soviets' ability to provide electricity for the whole of the USSR. In spite of an outward show of strength and prosperity, for most Soviet people poverty and suffering continued long after the end of the war.

THE WARSAW PACT

Another of Stalin's monuments was the division of Europe, clearer than ever at his death and confirmed in the next few years. The Western half was by 1953 substantially rebuilt, thanks to American economic support. The Federal Republic and the German Democratic Republic (GDR) moved further and further apart. On two successive days in March 1954 the Russians announced that the Eastern republic now possessed full sovereignty and the West German president signed the constitutional amendment permitting the rearmament of his country. In 1955 West Germany entered NATO; the Russian riposte was the Warsaw Pact, an alliance of its satellites. Berlin's future was still in doubt, but it was clear that the NATO powers would fight to resist changes in its status except by agreement. In the East, the GDR agreed to settle with old enemies: the line of the Oder-Neisse was to be the frontier with Poland. Hitler's dream of realizing the greater Germany of the nineteenth-century nationalists had ended in the obliteration of Bismarckian Germany. Historic Prussia was now ruled by revolutionary Communists, while the new West Germany was federal in structure, non-militarist in sentiment and dominated by Catholic and Social Democratic politicians whom Bismarck would have seen as "enemies of the state". So, without a peace treaty, the problem of containing the German power which had twice devastated Europe by war was settled for thirty-five years. Also in 1955 came the final definition of land frontiers between the European blocs, when Austria re-emerged as an independent state, the occupying allied forces being withdrawn, as were the last American and British troops from Trieste, with a settlement of the Italo-Yugoslav border dispute there.

THE EMERGENCE OF TWO ECONOMIC SYSTEMS

We cannot, of course, attribute to Stalin or any one person another division which was already spread worldwide after the establishment of Communism in China, that between what we may call capitalist and command (or would-be command) economies. Yet Stalin's policies helped to deepen it. Commercial relations between Soviet Russia and other countries had been encumbered by politics from the October Revolution onwards. There had followed the huge disruption of world trade after 1931 as the capitalist economies plunged into recession and sought salvation in protection (or, even, autarky). After 1945, though, all earlier divisions of the world market were transcended; two methods of organizing the distribution of scarce resources increasingly divided first the developed world and then a few other areas (of which the most important was constituted by China's stance in eastern Asia). The essential determinant of one system, the capitalist, was the market – though a market very different from that envisaged by the old liberal free trade ideology and in

The peace treaty with Austria is signed in 1955. Aware of its vulnerable position between Eastern and Western Europe, Austria declared itself neutral.

Post-war Germany and Central Europe

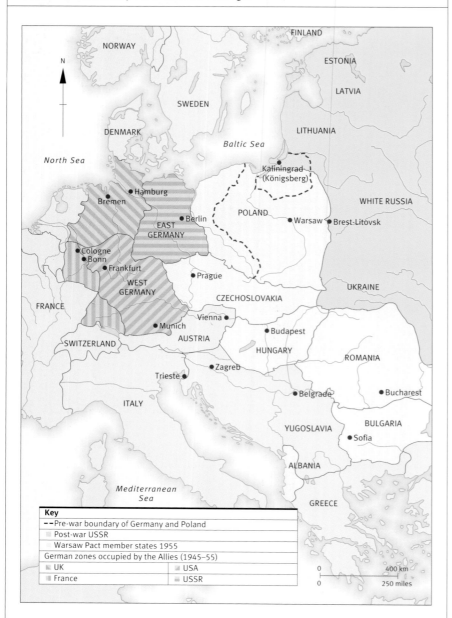

Key

- – – Pre-war boundary of Germany and Poland
- Post-war USSR
- Warsaw Pact member states 1955
- German zones occupied by the Allies (1945–55)

UK	USA
France	USSR

The Warsaw Pact was created as a reaction to the admission of a remilitarized West Germany into NATO. On 11 May, 1955, the Warsaw conference was opened, with representatives from the USSR, Poland, Hungary, Czechoslovakia, East Germany, Romania, Bulgaria and Albania. On 14 May, they signed the "treaty for friendship, cooperation and mutual aid". In an annex to the treaty, the unified high command for their armed forces was created, and the Soviet general Koniev was appointed to the post of commander-in-chief.

In this map showing the situation in 1955, the three western zones constitute the Federal Republic (West Germany), while the Russian zone is the German Democratic Republic (East Germany). Berlin remained under four-power occupation.

many ways a very imperfect one, tolerating a substantial degree of intervention through international agencies and agreement; in the Communist-controlled group of nations (and some others) political authority was intended to be the decisive economic factor. Trade between them continued, but on a severely restricted basis.

Neither system remained unchanged. Contacts between them multiplied as the years passed. None the less, they long offered alternative models for economic growth. Their competition was inflamed by the political struggles of the Cold War and actually helped to spread its antagonisms. This could not be a static situation. Before long the one system was much less completely dominated by the United States and the other somewhat less completely dominated by the Soviet Union than was the case in 1950. Both shared (though in far different degree) in the continuing economic growth of the 1950s and the 1960s, but were later to diverge as the market economies moved ahead more rapidly. The distinction between the two economic systems nevertheless remained a fundamental of world economic history from 1945 to the 1980s, shutting off some possibilities and suggesting others.

The entry of China to the world of what were called socialist economic systems was nevertheless at first seen almost purely in Cold War terms, and as a shift in strategic balances. Yet by the time of Stalin's death there were many other signs that the prophecy made by the South African statesman Smuts more than a quarter-century before that "the scene had shifted away from Europe to the Far East and the Pacific" had been realized. Although Germany continued to be the focus of Cold War strategy, Korea was the first dramatic evidence that the centre of gravity of world history was moving once again, this time from Europe to the Orient.

THE ASIAN REVOLUTION

THE COLLAPSE OF EUROPEAN POWER in Asia was bound to be followed by further changes as new Asian states came to be aware of their interests and power (or lack of it). Shape and unity given them by their former masters often did not long outlast the empires; the subcontinent of India lost its brief political unity at the very moment of decolonization; Malaysia and Indo-China were already before 1950 beginning to undergo important and not always welcome changes. Internal strains troubled some new nations; Indonesia's large Chinese communities had disproportionate weight and economic power and anything that happened in the new China might disturb them. Whatever their political circumstances, moreover, all these countries had fast-growing populations

and were economically backward. For many of them, therefore, the end of European domination now seems less of a turning-point than once thought. The biggest changes came later.

Europe's control of their destinies had for the most part been fitful. Though Europeans had swayed the fate of millions of Asians, and had influenced their lives for centuries, their civilization had touched the hearts and minds of few but the ruling élites. In Asia that civilization had to contend with deeper-rooted and more powerful traditions than anywhere else in the world. Asian cultures had not been (because they could not be) swept aside like those of pre-Columbian America. As in the Arab Islamic world, both the direct efforts of European and the indirect diffusion of European culture through self-imposed modernization faced formidable obstacles. The

Hindus take part in the Kumba Mela festival in India, which is alternately held in the holy cities of Hardwar, Allahabad, Ujjain and Nasik. Millions of pilgrims attend the festival every year, a sign of the continuing weight in Asia of ancient traditions, untouched by Western influence.

deepest layers of thought and behaviour often remained undisturbed even in some who believed themselves most emancipated from their past; nativities are still cast in educated Hindu families when children are born and marriages are contracted, and the Chinese Marxist draws on an unassailable sense of moral superiority grounded in age-old Chinese attitudes to the non-Chinese world.

TWO ASIAS

For the purpose of understanding Asia's recent role in world history two zones of Asian civilization are as distinct and significant as they have been for centuries. A western Asian sphere is bounded by the mountain ranges of northern India, the Burmese and Siamese highlands and the huge archipelago of which Indonesia is the major component. Its centre is the Indian Ocean and in its history the major cultural influences have been three: Hindu civilization spreading from India to the southeast, Islam (which also spread eastward across it), and the European impact, felt for fairly long periods through commercial and religious activity, and then for a much shorter era of political domination. The other sphere is East Asian, and is dominated by China. In large measure this is a function of the simple geographical fact of that country's huge mass, but the numbers and, sometimes, the migration of her people, and, more indirectly and variably, by China's cultural influence on the East Asian periphery – above all, Japan, Korea and Indo-China – all form part of the explanation. In this zone, direct European political domination had never compared with that further west in Asia, either in extent or duration.

The fakir, or holy man, remains one of the symbols of traditional India.

INDIA

IT WAS EASY TO LOSE SIGHT of the important differences between eastern and western Asia, as of much else imposed by history, in the troubled years after 1945. In both zones there were countries which seemed to follow the same road. Both provided examples of angry rejections of the West, expressed in Western language and appealing to world opinion on long-familiar lines. India, for example, absorbed within a few years both the princely states which had survived the Raj and the subcontinent's remaining French and Portuguese enclaves in the name of a truculent nationalism which owed little to Indian native tradition. Soon, the Indian security forces were energetically suppressing any threat of separatism or regional autonomy within the new republic. Perhaps this should not have been surprising. Indian independence was, on the Indian side, the work of a Western-educated élite which had imported the ideas of nationalism – like those of equality and liberty – from the West, even if it had at first only sought equality and partnership with the Raj itself. A threat to that élite's position after 1947 could often be most easily (and sincerely) understood as a threat to an Indian nationhood which had in fact still to be created.

PROBLEMS FACING THE NEW GOVERNMENT

The rulers of the newly independent India had inherited, to a degree often overlooked, many of the aspirations and institutions of the British Raj. Ministerial structures, constitutional conventions, division of powers between central and provincial authorities, the apparatus of public order and security were all taken over, stamped with republican insignia, and continued to operate much as before 1947. The dominant and explicit ideology of government was a moderate and bureaucratic socialism in the current British mode, and this was not far removed in spirit from the public-works-and-enlightenment despotism-by-delegation of the Raj in its last years. The realities which faced India's rulers included a deep conservative reluctance among local notables who controlled votes to disturb traditional privilege at any level below that of the former princes. Yet awesome problems faced India – population growth, economic backwardness, poverty (the average annual per capita income of Indians in 1950 was $55), illiteracy, social, tribal, religious division, and great expectations of what independence ought to bring. It was clear that major change was needed.

The installation of the new constitution in 1950 did nothing to change these facts, some of which would not begin to exercise their full weight until at least the second decade of the new India's existence. Even at the end of the century, much of life in rural India still goes on virtually as it has always done (war, natural disaster, and the banditry of exploiting rulers permitting). This implied gross poverty for some. In 1960, over a third of the rural poor were living on less than a dollar a

Nehru (1889–1964) is shown here on the second anniversary of Independence.

A street in the Indian city of Agra throngs with cycles, motorcycles and pedestrians. Unlike that of more highly industrialized countries, India's agricultural revolution is still incomplete and has hardly helped to feed its rapidly expanding population. Because the birth-rate is high, the growth of the cities has caused only a minimal drop in the size of the rural population.

week (and, at the same time, half the urban population earned less than enough to maintain the official minimum daily calorie intake required for health). Economic progress had been swallowed by population growth. In the circumstances it is hardly surprising that the rulers of India should have incorporated in the constitution provisions for emergency powers as drastic as any ever enjoyed by a British viceroy, providing as they did for preventative detention and the suspension of individual rights, to say nothing of the suspension of state government and the submission of states to Union control under what was called "President's Rule".

TENSION BETWEEN INDIA AND PAKISTAN

The weaknesses and uneasiness of a "new nation" made things worse when India quarrelled with her neighbour, Pakistan. It was first seriously evident over Kashmir, where a Hindu prince ruled over a majority of Muslim subjects. Fighting began there as early as 1947, when the Muslims tried to bring about union with Pakistan; the Maharaja asked for Indian help and joined the Indian republic. To complicate things further, the Muslim spokesmen of Kashmir were themselves divided. India refused to hold the plebiscite recommended by the United Nations Security Council; two-thirds of Kashmir then remained in Indian hands to ensure a running sore in Indo-Pakistani relations. Fighting stopped in 1949, only to break out again in 1965–6 and 1969–70. The issue had by then been further complicated by demarcation disputes and quarrels over the use of the Indus waters. In 1971 there was more fighting between the two states when East Pakistan, a Muslim, but Bengali-speaking, region broke away to form a new state, Bangladesh, under Indian patronage (thus showing that religious unity alone was not enough to constitute a viable nation). It soon faced economic problems even greater than those of India or Pakistan.

POLITICAL ALIGNMENT

In these troubled passages, India's leaders showed great ambitions (perhaps going at times so far as a wish to reunite the subcontinent) and sometimes blatant disregard of the interests of other peoples (such as the Nagas). The irritation aroused by Indian aspirations was moreover further complicated by the Cold War. India's leader, Nehru, had quickly insisted that India would not take sides. In the 1950s, this meant that India had warmer relations with Russia and Communist China than with the United States; indeed, Nehru appeared to relish opportunities of criticizing American action, which helped to convince some sympathizers of India's credentials as a progressive, peaceful, "non-aligned"

The problems of the young state of Bangladesh have been exacerbated by a series of natural disasters. The cyclones that regularly devastate the country also cause floods, such as this one in 1988.

democracy. It came as all the greater a shock, therefore, to them and to the Indian public to learn in 1959 that Nehru's government had been quarrelling with the Chinese about the northern borders for the previous three years without saying so. At the end of 1962, large-scale fighting began. Nehru took the improbable step of asking the Americans for military aid and, even more improbably, of receiving it at the same time as he also took it (in the form of aeroplane engines) from Russia.

Logically, the young Pakistan had not courted the same friends as India. She was in 1947 much weaker than her neighbour, with only a tiny trained civil service (Hindus had joined the old Indian Civil Service in much larger numbers than Muslims). She was also divided geographically in two from the start, and almost at once had lost her ablest leader, Jinnah. Even under the Raj, Muslim leaders had always (and perhaps realistically) shown less confidence in democratic forms than

From 1958 to 1973 Pakistan was run by military dictatorships, an expression of the dominant Muslim oligarchy. From 1973 to 1977 Zufilkar Ali Bhutto (1928–1979) tried to establish a civil government, but a coup resulted in yet another military dictatorship. In 1988 Ali Bhutto's daughter, Benazir Bhutto (b.1953), pictured here, became the first elected prime minister of Pakistan, ruling until 1990, effectively on the basis of an agreement with the army.

Congress; usually, Pakistan has been ruled by authoritarian soldiers who have sought to ensure military survival against India, economic development, including land reform, and the safeguarding of Islamic ways.

THE THIRD WORLD

Whereas India's friends in the West were sometimes disappointed by her politics after independence, less had been expected of Pakistan. It always helped to distance her from India that she was formally Muslim while her neighbour was constitutionally secular and non-confessional (at first sight a seemingly "Western" stance, but one not hard to reconcile with India's predominantly Hindu and syncretic cultural tradition). This was to lead Pakistan towards increasing Islamic regulation of its internal affairs. Religious difference, though, affected Pakistan's foreign relations less than did the Cold War,

which itself brought further confusion to Asian politics when a new association of professedly neutralist or "non-aligned" nations emerged after a meeting of representatives of twenty-nine African and Asian states at Bandung in Indonesia in 1955. Most delegations other than China's were from lands which had been part of the colonial empires. From Europe, Yugoslavia was soon to join them. They were also poor and needy, more suspicious of the United States than of Russia, and more attracted to China than to either. These came to be called the "Third World" nations, a term apparently coined by a French journalist in a conscious reminiscence of the legally underprivileged French "Third Estate" of 1789 which had provided much of the driving-force of the French Revolution. The implication was that such nations were disregarded by the great powers, and excluded from the economic privileges of the developed countries. Plausible though this might sound, the expression "Third World" actually

The Bandung Conference

Held in Indonesia in 1955, the Bandung Conference was attended by representatives from 29 countries that had recently gained independence, with the aim of analysing their common political, economic and cultural problems. The following were affirmed at the end of the conference: the independence and equality of the Afro–Asian countries; a condemnation of colonialism; respect for human rights; a policy of non-intervention in the internal affairs of other countries; non-participation in collective agreements favouring the individual interests of a particular power; the right of every nation to defend itself; and the creation of the Non-Aligned Countries Movement.

However, the policy of strict neutrality, advocated by Tito, was unlikely to be implemented. The radical countries – mostly African ones supported by Cuba – had aggressive policies giving priority to the anti-imperialist struggle. On the other hand, the moderate countries, led by India, emphasized the need to solve the East–West problems.

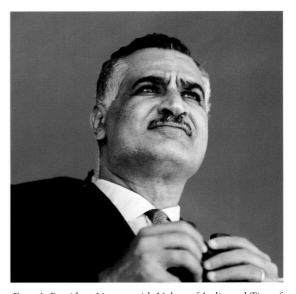

Egypt's President Nasser, with Nehru of India and Tito of Yugoslavia, was a key leader at the Bandung Conference.

In order to continue with the self-sufficient economic model that Tito (shown here addressing a rally in Skopje in 1953) had set up for Yugoslavia, the Yugoslav government had to seek aid from the West. Yugoslavia received large loans from the United States and the International Monetary Fund (IMF), which increased tension between Belgrade and the other countries in the Communist bloc. Tito tried to develop a policy of neutrality and non-alignment in international affairs.

masked important differences between the members of that group and in their individual relations with the developed world. Not surprisingly, the coherence of Third World politics was not to prove very enduring. Since 1955 more people have been killed in wars and civil wars within that world than in conflicts external to it.

THE COLD WAR IN ASIA

Ten years after the end of the Second World War Bandung forced the great powers to recognize that the weak had power if they could mobilize it. They bore this in mind as they looked for allies in the Cold War. By 1960 there were already clear signs that Russian and Chinese interests might diverge and each sought the leadership of the underdeveloped and uncommitted. At first this emerged obliquely in the disguise of differing attitudes to the Yugoslavs; it was in the end to be a worldwide contest. One early result was the paradox that as time passed Pakistan drew closer to China (in spite of a treaty with the United States) and India closer to Russia. When the United States declined to supply arms during her 1965 war with India, Pakistan asked for Chinese help. She got much less than she hoped, but this was early evidence of a new fluidity which began to mark international affairs in the 1960s.

No more than the USSR or China could the United States ignore this. Indeed, the Cold War was to produce an ironical change in the Americans' role in Asia; from being the patrons of the anti-colonialism which had done so much to dismantle their allies' empires, they began in some areas almost to appear as their successors, though in the East Asian rather than in the Indian Ocean sphere, where long and unrewarded efforts were made to placate an ungrateful India (before 1960 she received more economic aid from the United States than any other country).

INDEPENDENT INDONESIA

ONE EXAMPLE of the new difficulties facing great powers was provided by Indonesia. Its vast sprawl encompasses many peoples, often with widely diverging interests. The basic culture of the Sumatrans and Javanese is Hindu, but, at least formally, Indonesia also has the largest Muslim population under one government in the world. Arab traders had brought Islam to Indonesia's peoples from the thirteenth century onwards, and more than four-fifths of the Indonesian population is reckoned now to be Muslim, although traditional animism perhaps matters as much in determining their behaviour. Indonesia also has a well-entrenched Chinese community, enjoying in the colonial period a preponderant share of wealth and administrative jobs. The departure of the Dutch released communal tensions from the discipline an alien ruler had imposed just as the usual post-colonial problems – overpopulation, poverty, inflation – began to be felt.

SUKARNO IS DEPOSED

In the 1950s the central government of the new republic was increasingly resented; by 1957 it had faced armed rebellion in Sumatra and unrest elsewhere. The time-honoured device of distracting opposition with nationalist excitement (directed against a continual Dutch presence in west New Guinea) did not work any more; popular support for Sukarno was not rebuilt. His government had already moved away from the liberal forms adopted at the birth of the new state and he leant more and more on Soviet support. In 1960 parliament was dismissed, and in 1963 Sukarno was named president for life. Yet the United States, fearing he might turn to China for help, long stood by him. This enabled him to swallow up (to the irritation of the Dutch) a would-be independent state which had emerged from west New Guinea. Sukarno then turned on the new federation of Malaysia, put together in 1957 from fragments of the British Empire in Southeast Asia.

Communist prisoners at the notorious Salembra jail in Indonesia are given a lesson in politics as part of their "re-education".

With British help, Malaysia mastered Indonesian attacks on Borneo, Sarawak and the Malaysian mainland. Although he still enjoyed American patronage (at one moment, President Kennedy's brother appeared in London to support his cause), this setback seems to have been the turning-point for Sukarno. Exactly what happened is still obscure, but when food shortages and inflation went out of control, a coup was attempted (it failed) behind which, said the leaders of the army, were the Communists. It is at least possible that Indonesia was intended by Mao to play a major part in the export of revolution; the Communist Party which Sukarno had tried to balance against other politicians was at one time alleged to be the third largest in the world. Whether or not a Communist takeover was intended, though, the economic crisis was exploited by those who feared one. The popular and traditional Indonesian shadow theatres were for months seasoning the old Hindu epics which were their staple material with plentiful political allusions and overtones of coming change. When the storm broke, in 1965, the army stood back ostentatiously while popular massacre removed the Communists to whom Sukarno might have turned. Estimates of the number killed vary between a quarter of and a half a million. Sukarno himself was duly set aside the following year. A solidly anti-Communist régime then took power which broke off diplomatic relations with China (they were not to be renewed until 1990). It has kept some of the losers of 1965 in jail until the present day, taking a few out from time to time to be hanged as evidence of resolute prosecution of the struggle against Communism and, no doubt, *pour encourager les autres*.

Paradoxically (and almost incomprehensibly, given Indonesia's problems), American support for Sukarno had reflected the belief

that strong, prosperous national states were the best bulwarks against Communism. The history of Far Eastern Asia in the last forty years can be read so as to offer support for that principle, but its successful expression in American policy was always far from unqualified. Difficulty lay in its practical application.

CHINESE POWER REASSERTED

BY 1960, THE DOMINANT strategical fact east of Singapore was the re-creation of Chinese power. South Korea and Japan had successfully resisted Communism but they benefited from the Chinese Revolution; it gave them leverage against the West. Just as East Asians had always held off Europeans more successfully than the Indian Ocean countries, they have showed after 1947 an ability to buttress their independence in both communist and non-communist forms, and not to succumb to direct Chinese manipulation. It is difficult not to link this, ironically, to the deep and many-faceted conservatism of societies which had for centuries drawn on Chinese example. In their discipline, capacity for constructive social effort, disregard for the individual, respect for authority and hierarchy, and deep self-awareness as members of civilizations proudly distinct from the West, the East Asians drew on something much deeper than the Chinese Revolution; indeed, that revolution is only comprehensible against the background dominated by that something.

THE CHINESE RECOVERY STARTS

We may begin with the Chinese Revolution's victory and installation in power in 1949. Peking (Beijing) was once more the capital of China. Some thought this showed that China's leaders might again be more aware of pressure from her land frontiers in the north than of the threat from the sea which had faced her for more than a century. However this may be, the Soviet Union was the first state to recognize the new China, closely followed by the United Kingdom, India and Burma. Given Cold War preoccupations elsewhere and the circumstances of the Nationalist collapse, the new China in fact faced no real threat from the outside. Her rulers could concentrate on the long overdue and immensely difficult task of modernization; the Nationalists, cooped up in Taiwan, could be disregarded, though for the moment irremovable. When a major threat appeared, as the United Nations forces approached the Yalu River frontier of Manchuria in 1950, the Chinese reaction was strong and immediate: they sent a large army to Korea. But the main preoccupation of China's new rulers was the

The former British Crown Colony of Singapore acquired a vigorous new autonomous government in 1959. In 1963 Singapore joined the Federation of Malaysia, but broke away as an independent republic in 1965. It is now an active commercial enclave, boasting one of the best communications networks in Southeast Asia, and has become one of the so-called "Asian Tigers".

internal state of the country. Poverty was universal. Disease and malnutrition were widespread. Material and physical construction and reconstruction were overdue, population pressure on land was as serious as ever, and the moral and ideological void presented by the collapse of the *ancien régime* over the preceding century had to be filled.

The peasants were the starting-point. Here 1949 is not a very significant date. Since the 1920s land reform had been carried out largely by the peasants themselves in areas the Communists dominated. By 1956 China's farms were collectivized in a social transformation of the villages which was intended to give control of the new units to their inhabitants. The essential change was the overthrow of local village leaders and landlords; it was often violent and such persons must have made up a large number of the 800,000 Chinese later reported by Mao to have been "liquidated" in the first five years of the

Chinese children work in the fields in 1949. On the eve of the revolution, 50 per cent of the land in China was owned by a mere 4 per cent of landowners, powerful magnates to whom most peasants were permanently indebted.

People's Republic. Meanwhile industrialization was also pressed forward, with Russian help, the only source from which China could draw. The model chosen, too, was the Soviet one: a Five Year Plan was announced and launched in 1953. It was a remarkable success. By 1956 it had produced an increase in the Chinese net domestic product proportionately greater than the increase in the production of food. A contrast with India was emerging which was to grow much more striking.

An agricultural commune near Peking (Beijing) is shown. Many such collective farms were set up following Mao's land reforms of the 1950s.

FOREIGN AFFAIRS

By 1956 China was once more a major influence abroad, though her independence was long masked by the superficial unity of the Communist bloc and her continued exclusion from UNO at the insistence of the United States. A Sino-Soviet treaty in 1950 was interpreted – especially in the United States – as evidence that China was entering the Cold War. Certainly, the régime was Communist and talked revolution and anti-colonialism, and its choices were bound to be confined by the parameters of the Cold War. Yet in a longer perspective more traditional concerns now seem evident in Chinese Communist policy from the start. At a very early point, there was visible a concern to re-establish Chinese power within the area it had always tended to fill up.

The security of Manchuria is by itself enough to explain Chinese military intervention in Korea, but the peninsula had also long been an area of dispute between imperial China and Japan. A Chinese occupation of Tibet in 1951 was another incursion into an area which had for centuries been under

Chinese suzerainty. But from the start the most vociferous demand made for regaining control of the Chinese periphery was for the eviction of the KMT government from Taiwan, seized in 1895 by the Japanese and only briefly restored in 1945 to control by the mainland. By 1955, a United States government was so deeply committed to the support of the KMT régime there that the president announced that the United States would protect not merely the island itself but the smaller islands near the Chinese coast which were thought essential to its defence. About this issue and against a psychological background provided by a sense of inexplicable rebuff from a China long patronized by American philanthropy and missionary effort, the interest of Americans in Chinese affairs tended to crystallize for over a decade. So obsessively did it do so, that the KMT tail seemed at times to wag the American dog. Conversely, during the 1950s, both India and Russia supported Peking over Taiwan, insisting that the matter was one of Chinese internal affairs; it cost them nothing to do so. Sensation was therefore all the greater when the next decade brought fighting between China and these two countries.

CHINA AND INDIA

The quarrel with India grew out of the Chinese occupation of Tibet. When the Chinese further tightened their grasp on that country in 1959, Indian policy still seemed basically sympathetic to China. An attempt by Tibetan exiles to set up a government on Indian soil was stifled. But by then territorial disputes had begun, and had already led to clashes. The Chinese announced that they did not recognize a border with India along lines drawn by a British-Tibetan negotiation in 1914 and never formally accepted by any Chinese

A steelworker in a factory in Wuhan is pictured. The first Five-Year Plan plunged China into socialism, with the nationalization of both heavy and light industry.

This scene from the mountainous landscape of Tibet shows Mount Everest in the background and the Rongbuk monastery in the foreground. Chinese occupation of this thinly populated Himalayan country led to a brief war with India in 1962.

government. Forty-odd years' usage was hardly significant against China's millennial historical memory. As a result, there was much heavier fighting in the autumn of 1962, when Nehru demanded a Chinese withdrawal from the disputed zone. The Indians did badly, though fighting ceased, at the end of the year, on the initiative of the Chinese.

CHINA AND THE SOVIET UNION

Early in 1963, a startled world suddenly heard the Soviet Union bitterly denounced by the Chinese Communists. On the one hand, said the Chinese, the Russians had helped India, and on the other, they had, in a hostile gesture, cut off economic and military aid to China three years earlier. The second charge showed there were complex origins to this quarrel, but by no means went to the root of the matter. Some Chinese Communists (Mao among them) could, after all, remember what had happened when Chinese interests had been subordinated to the international interest of Communism, as interpreted by Moscow, in the 1920s. Since that time there had always been a tension in the leadership of the Chinese Party between Soviet and native forces. Mao himself represented the latter. Unfortunately, such subtleties were difficult to disentangle because Chinese resentment of Soviet policy had to be presented to the rest of the world in Marxist jargon. Since the new leadership in Russia was engaged at the time in the dismantling of the Stalin myth, this almost accidentally led the Chinese to sound more Stalinist than Stalin in their public pronouncements even when they were pursuing non-Stalinist policies.

In 1963, it would also have been of utility to non-Chinese observers to recall an even more remote past to Sino-Soviet relations. Long before the foundation of the CCP, the

Collectivization in China

Before culminating in the commune – the maximum level of collectivization – Chinese agrarian development went through several stages. In 1955, the "semi-socialist production cooperatives" appeared, which brought together 30 or 40 families; in 1956, the "socialist cooperatives" formed groups of between 100 and 300 families, divided into brigades and teams; and finally came the communes.

During the Great Leap Forward 740,000 socialist cooperatives were grouped together into 26,000 communes with an average of 4,634 families in each. But from 1962, when this type of organization was deemed to be too large to manage and inefficient, the 26,000 communes were converted into 74,000, each of which encompassed only a third of the land of the old communes and employed just one third of the workforce.

Within the commune, the smallest cell was the production team. Each team worked about 15 to 20 hectares of land and supplemented its production by food grown on private plots and animal husbandry.

A production brigade was made up of seven or eight teams, which were coordinated to carry out communal work. The commune itself was comprised of 12 or 13 brigades. Most communes had an important social services centre, which provided secondary education and hospital care. It also administered tax collection, public safety, the civil register and the commercialization of excess production.

In spite of the highly structured nature of their organization, Chinese communes were far from uniform, owing to differences in the environmental conditions in which they were located and the varying quality of their links to urban markets.

The first Chinese communes consisted of seven or eight families who shared tools and draught animals. The members of these "Mutual Aid Work Teams" later shared tractors, such as the one driven by these men in the Gao Kan commune in Senyang.

Chinese Revolution had been a movement of national regeneration. One of its primary aims had been the recovery from the foreigners of China's control over her own destiny. Among these foreigners, the Russians were pre-eminent. Their record of encroachment upon the Chinese sphere went back to Peter the Great. It had continued all through the tsarist to the Soviet era. A protectorate over Tannu Tuva had been established in 1914 by the tsars, but the area was annexed by the Soviet Union in 1944. In 1945 Russian armies entered Manchuria and north China and thus reconstituted the tsarist Far East of 1900; they remained in Sinkiang until 1949, in Port Arthur until 1955. In Mongolia they left behind a satellite Mongolian People's Republic they had set up in the 1920s. With something like 4,500 miles of shared frontier (if Mongolia is included), the potential for dispute along its huge length was immense.

Mao Tse-tung's personal experience must also have counted for much. Although his later intellectual formation had been Marxist and although he found its categories helpful in explaining his country's predicament, he appears always to have diluted them with a certain pragmatism. He escaped the Marxist dogma of the Bolshevik period because of a firm belief in the lessons of experience, and advocated a sinicized Marxism which envisaged a society unlike that of Soviet Russia as well as non-capitalist. His attitude to knowledge and ideas was predominantly utilitarian and moralistic, and thus very much in the

Chinese tradition. The basis of his world view, rather than the bloodless categories of the dialectic, appears to have been a classification of phenomena into contending forces on which human will-power could at any moment play to bring about morally valuable and creative change.

MAO TSE-TUNG'S CHINA

MAO'S RELATIONSHIP with his party had not always been smooth. His first opportunity had come when his policy towards the peasantry provided a way ahead after disaster had overtaken urban communism. After a temporary setback in the early 1930s he was from about 1935 virtually supreme within the party. Rural influences were on top. A way was also opened for Mao to future enormous international influence; the notion of a protracted revolutionary war, waged from the countryside and carried into the towns, looked promising in other parts of the world where the orthodox Marxist belief that industrial development was needed to create a revolutionary proletariat was not persuasive.

The Sino-Soviet conflict announced in 1963 in the end entangled the whole Communist world. It was inflamed by Russian tactlessness. The Soviet leaders seem to have been as careless as any Western imperialists of the emotions of Asiatic allies: Khrushchev once revealingly remarked that when touring in China, he and other Russians "used to laugh at their primitive forms of organization". The withdrawal of Soviet economic and technical help in 1960 had been a grave affront just when natural disasters – floods are said by official Chinese sources to have drowned a hundred and fifty million acres of agricultural land – had followed the collapse of an economic offensive launched in 1958 by

Mao, the "Great Leap Forward". The object of the "leap" appears to have been to decentralize the economy into "communes", of which there were some twenty-five thousand, thus repudiating centralized planning on the Russian model with its bureaucratic dangers, as well as calling directly upon the participation of local forces from which the régime had previously benefited. It failed badly. Mao's standing suffered.

GROWING CHINESE CONFIDENCE

Mao's rivals came together to put the economy back on the road to modernization again. One striking symbol was the explosion of a Chinese nuclear weapon in 1964, an expensive admission card to a very exclusive club. It was probably more important, at least immediately, that the régime managed to avoid crippling famine and kept the loyalty of the people. Though more slowly than in the

The split between the Soviet and the Chinese Communist parties came during the 23rd Congress of the Soviet Communist Party in October 1961. In December 1962, Khrushchev, pictured here, publicly attacked Peking for allowing the imperialist enclaves of Macau and Hong Kong to exist on Chinese territory. Throughout 1963, the two parties sent mutual accusations to each other in the form of open letters.

past, the Chinese population had continued to rise to even more colossal totals. Five hundred and ninety million has been thought a reasonable estimate for 1950; twenty-five years later, it was 835 million. Though China's share of world population may have sometimes been higher in the past – perhaps she contained nearly 40 per cent of humanity on the eve of the Taiping rebellion – she was in the 1960s stronger than ever before. Her leaders even talked as if they were unmoved by the possibility of nuclear war; Chinese would survive in greater numbers than the peoples of other countries. There were signs that the USSR was alarmed by the presence of such a demographic mass on the border of her most thinly populated regions. China, after all, is not only one of the most highly, but also one of the most densely populated countries in the world.

THE CULTURAL REVOLUTION

In the 1960s, the revolution seemed not to have lost the dynamism which the Party strove to keep alive. Much turned on the fear of what had happened in the USSR, where substantial change and relaxation seemed to follow in the decade after Stalin's death and, as was later to become common knowledge, deep corruption and conservatism gradually took hold of the Party and the bureaucrats. The fear that something similar might happen in China lay behind the "Cultural Revolution" of 1966–9. This huge upheaval, sweeping through Party and administration, was an attempt to offset the danger that a new ruling class would emerge, and a consequence also of the re-establishment of Mao's prestige. The cult of Maoism was to be revitalized for a new generation. One way in which Cultural Revolution expressed itself was, oddly, by closing universities. Physical labour was demanded of all citizens in order to change traditional attitudes towards intellectuals. The new emphasis was upon self-sacrifice and subordination to the thought of Mao Tse-tung. By 1968 the country had been turned upside-down by young "Red Guards" fighting entrenched officialdom and there were signs that Mao himself believed things had gone too far. After the army re-established order and instituted new cadres a Party congress reconfirmed his leadership, but he had again failed.

The moral preoccupation of this mysterious episode is very striking. It was, in a way, an attempt (Mao's last, as it turned out) to give his ideas a spiritual meaning for a new generation. Clearly Mao personally felt a danger that the revolution might congeal and lose the moral élan which had carried it so far. In seeking to protect it, old ideas had to go. This should not seem surprising. Of the great revolutions of world history, the Chinese has been unquestionably one of the most far-reaching. It had to be. Society, government and economy were enmeshed and integrated with one another into a whole system in China as nowhere else. The traditional prestige of intellectuals and scholars still embodied the old order, just as had the examination system whose abolition more than fifty years earlier had been one of the announcements that a real revolution and not just a change of régime was under way in the most unchanging society on earth. The "demotion" of intellectuals was urged as a necessary consequence of making a new China. It is in this perspective that Chinese Communism's achievement and direction stand out from the mystifying welter of events which bemuse the foreign observer. Deliberate attacks on family authority, for example, were not merely attempts by a suspicious régime to encourage informers and delation, but attacks on the most conservative of all Chinese institutions. Similarly, the advancement of women and propaganda to discourage early marriage had dimensions going beyond "progressive" feminist ideas or population control; they were an assault on the past such as no other revolution had ever made, for in China the past meant a role for women far inferior to anything to be found in pre-revolutionary America, France or Russia. The attacks on Party leaders which accused them of flirtation with Confucian ideas were much more than the jibes which comparable attacks would have been in Western countries; indeed, they could not have occurred in the West, where no vision of a past to be rejected which was so total could exist after centuries of cultural pluralism.

THE NATURE OF THE CHINESE REVOLUTION

Rejection is only half the story of the Chinese Revolution. More than two thousand years of a continuity stretching back to the Ch'in and perhaps further also lives behind it. One clue is the role of authority in it. For all its cost and cruelty, it was a heroic endeavour; in scale it is matched only by such gigantic social efforts as the spread of Islam, or Europe's assault on the world in early modern times. Yet it was different from such movements because it was at least in intention centrally controlled and directed. It is a paradox of the Chinese Revolution that it rests on popular fervour but is unimaginable without conscious direction from a state inheriting all the mysterious prestige of the traditional bearers of the Mandate of Heaven. Chinese tradition respects authority and gives it a moral endorsement which has long been hard to find in the West. No more than any other great state could China shake off its history, and as a result the Communist régime

sometimes has a paradoxically conservative appearance. No large society had for so long driven home to its peoples the lessons that the individual mattered less than the collective whole, that authority could rightfully command the services of millions at any cost to themselves in order to carry out great works for the good of the state, that authority is unquestionable so long as it is exercised for the common good. The notion of opposition is distasteful to the Chinese because it

A flamboyant parade is held in Peking in August 1968, during the Cultural Revolution.

Chinese people recite texts from the Little Red Book, in which Mao stressed the need to reduce urban–rural differences and the importance of "perpetual revolution".

suggests social disruption; that implies the rejection of the kind of revolution involved in the adoption of Western individualism, though not of collective radicalism.

Mao fitted Chinese popular tradition. The régime over which he presided benefited from the Chinese past as well as destroying it, because Mao was easily comprehensible within its idea of authority. He was presented as a ruler-sage, as much a teacher as a politician; Western commentators were amused by the status given to his thoughts by the omnipresence of the Little Red Book (in the West after the Protestant Reformation similar extravagant adulation was sometimes given to the Bible), but the utterances of great teachers have always commanded respect in China. Mao was the spokesman of a moral doctrine which was presented as the core of society, just as Confucianism had been. There was also something traditional in Mao's artistic interests; he was admired by the people as a poet and his poems won the respect of qualified judges. In China power has always been sanctioned by the notion that the ruler did good things for his people and sustained accepted values. Mao's actions could be read in such a way.

WAR IN INDO-CHINA

The weight of the past was evident in Chinese foreign policies, too. Though it came to patronize revolution all over the world, China's main concern was with the Far East and, in particular, with Indo-China, a traditionally tributary country. There, Russian and Chinese policy again diverged. After the Korean War the Chinese began to supply arms to the Communist guerrilla forces in Vietnam for what was less a struggle against colonialism – that was decided already – than about what should follow it. In 1953 the French had given up both Cambodia and Laos. In 1954 they lost at a base called Dien Bien Phu a battle decisive both for French prestige and for the French electorate's will to fight. After this, it was impossible for the French to maintain themselves in the Red River delta. A conference at Geneva agreed to partition Vietnam between a South Vietnamese government and the Communists who had come to dominate the North, pending elections which might reunite the country. The elections never took place. Instead, there soon opened in Indo-China what was to become the fiercest phase since 1945 of the Asian war against the West begun in 1941.

The Western contenders were no longer the former colonial powers (the French had gone home and the British had problems enough elsewhere), but the Americans; on the other side was a mixture of the Indo-Chinese Communists, Nationalists and reformers supported by the Chinese and Russians. American anti-colonialism and the belief that the United States should support indigenous governments led it to back the South Vietnamese as it backed South Koreans and Filipinos. Unfortunately neither in Laos nor South Vietnam, nor, in the end, in Cambodia, did there emerge régimes of unquestioned legitimacy in the eyes of those they ruled.

Population pressure and post-war recovery in South and East Asia

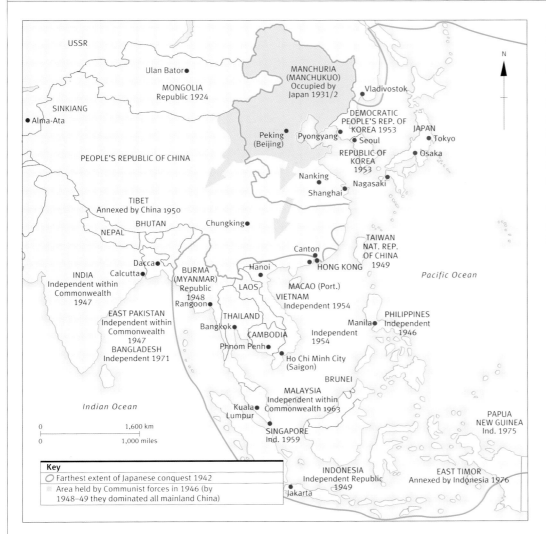

Although Chinese culture has been disseminated over the area shown on this map for centuries, that vast nation has had political influence over much of southern and eastern Asia. Only in the last couple of centuries was the region divided into areas of major European influence. Japan, which was particularly strong following the 19th-century Meiji Restoration, has also exerted a strong influence in the area.

Since the end of the Second World War, most southern and eastern Asian countries have gained independence from their old colonial rulers.

Key
⊘ Farthest extent of Japanese conquest 1942
▨ Area held by Communist forces in 1946 (by 1948–49 they dominated all mainland China)

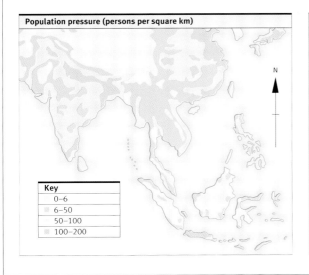

Population pressure (persons per square km)

Key
| 0–6 |
| 6–50 |
| 50–100 |
| 100–200 |

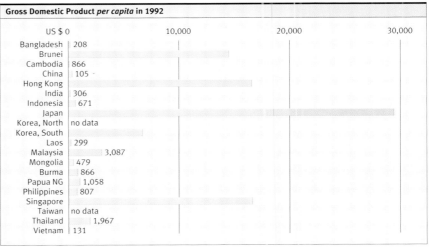

Gross Domestic Product per capita in 1992

	US $ 0	10,000	20,000	30,000
Bangladesh	208			
Brunei				
Cambodia	866			
China	105			
Hong Kong				
India	306			
Indonesia	671			
Japan				
Korea, North	no data			
Korea, South				
Laos	299			
Malaysia	3,087			
Mongolia	479			
Burma	866			
Papua NG	1,058			
Philippines	807			
Singapore				
Taiwan	no data			
Thailand	1,967			
Vietnam	131			

American support for South Vietnam would eventually spill over to neighbouring Cambodia. There the government tried to match the ferocity of the Communist guerrilla organization the Khmer Rouge. The heads of guerrillas are shown being carried from a battle zone.

American patronage merely identified them with the Western enemy so disliked in East Asia. American support also tended to remove the incentive to carry out reforms which would have united people behind these régimes, above all in Vietnam, where de facto partition did not produce good or stable government in the South. While Buddhists and Roman Catholics quarrelled bitterly and the peasants were more and more alienated from the régime by the failure of land reform, an

apparently corrupt ruling class seemed able to survive government after government. This benefited the Communists. They sought reunification on their own terms and maintained from the North support for the Communist underground movement in the South, the Vietcong.

By 1960 the Vietcong had won control of much of the South. This was the background to a momentous decision taken by the American president, John Kennedy, in 1962, to send not only financial and material help but also 4,000 American "advisers" to help the South Vietnam government put its military house in order. It was the first step towards what Truman had been determined to avoid, the involvement of the United States in a major war on the mainland of Asia (and, in the end, the loss of more than 50,000 American lives).

JAPAN IN 1945

ANOTHER OF WASHINGTON'S responses to Cold War in Asia had been to safeguard as long as possible the special position arising from the American occupation of Japan. This was virtually a monopoly, with only token participation by British Commonwealth forces. It had been possible because of the Soviet delay in declaring war on Japan and the speed of Japan's surrender. Stalin was taken by surprise. The Americans firmly rejected later Soviet requests for a share in an occupation Soviet power had done nothing to bring about, and the results were to be startling. The United States provided the last great example of Western paternalism in Asia and the Japanese once more demonstrated their astonishing gift for learning from others only what they wished to learn while safeguarding their own society against unsettling change.

Nineteen forty-five forced Japan spiritually into a twentieth century she had already entered technologically. Defeat confronted her people with deep and troubling problems of national identity and purpose. The westernization of the Meiji era had led to the dream of "Asia for the Asians". In its Japanese version, this idea was now blown away by defeat. It had really been a kind of Japanese Monroe doctrine, underpinned by the anti-Western sentiment so widespread in the Far East and cloaking imperialism. The slogan was given meaning in a different sense after 1945 by the rolling back of colonialism. That left Japan with no obvious and creditable Asian role. True, at that moment she seemed unlikely for a long time to have the power for one. Moreover, the war's demonstration of Japan's vulnerability had been a great shock; like the United Kingdom she had depended on control of the surface of the sea, and the loss of it had doomed her. Then there were the other results of defeat; the loss of territory to Russia on Sakhalin and the Kurile islands and the occupation by the Americans.

Finally, there was vast material and human destruction to repair.

JAPANESE RECOVERY

On the asset side, the Japanese in 1945 still had the unshaken central institution of the monarchy, whose prestige was undimmed and, indeed, had made the surrender possible. Many Japanese saw in the emperor Hirohito the man who had saved them from annihilation. The American commander in the Pacific, General MacArthur, wanted to maintain the monarchy as an instrument of a peaceful occupation. He took care to have a new Japanese constitution adopted before republican enthusiasts in the United States could interfere; he found it effective to argue that Japan should be helped economically in order to get it more quickly off the back of the American taxpayer. Japanese social cohesiveness and discipline was a great help, though for a time it seemed that the Americans might undermine this by the determination with

American troops cross a coral reef to reach a beach during their campaign in the Pacific (1942–1945). The sea battle in the Philippines was a disaster for the Japanese. Two Japanese naval chiefs of staff committed suicide when they saw that the Americans had taken the island of Saipan. As they advanced inland, American soldiers and marines were horrified to see women, old people and children throwing themselves off the cliffs, rather than face defeat.

The Showa emperor, Hirohito (1901–1989), the 124th sovereign from the reigning family, became regent when he was 20 years old, and was crowned emperor in 1926. In 1936, the totalitarian and militaristic Taisei Yokusankai party won the elections, and tried to manoeuvre the emperor away from political matters. However, after the atomic bombs had been dropped, Hirohito was able to get the government to agree to unconditional surrender. The United States kept Hirohito on the throne as the only guarantee for the pacification and rapid reconstruction of the country, and in 1946, by the terms of the new constitution, he duly became a constitutional monarch.

which they pressed democratic institutions upon the country. Some problems must have been eased by a major land reform in which about a third of the cultivated area of Japan passed from landowners' to cultivators' ownership. By 1951 that democratic education and careful demilitarization was deemed adequate for a peace treaty between Japan and most of her former opponents except the Russians and Nationalist Chinese (terms with them followed within a few years). Japan regained her full sovereignty, including a right to arms for defensive purposes, but gave up virtually all her former overseas possessions. Thus the Japanese emerged from the post-war era to resume control of their own affairs. An agreement with the United States provided for the maintenance of American forces on her soil. Confined to her own islands, and facing a China stronger and much better consolidated than for a century, Japan's position was not necessarily a disadvantageous one. In less than twenty years this much reduced status was, as it turned out, to be transformed again.

The Cold War had changed the implications of the American occupation even before 1951. Japan was separated from Russians and Chinese by, respectively, 10 and 500 miles of water. Korea, the old area of imperial rivalry, was only 150 miles away. The spread of the Cold War to Asia guaranteed Japan even better treatment from the Americans, now anxious to see her working convincingly as an example of democracy and capitalism, and also gave her the protection of the United States nuclear "umbrella". The Korean War made her important as a base, and galvanized the Japanese economy. The index of industrial production quickly went back up to the level of the 1930s. The United States promoted Japanese interests abroad through diplomacy. Finally, Japan long had no defence costs, since she was until 1951 forbidden to have any armed forces.

THE USA AND THE PACIFIC STATES

Japan's close connexion with the United States, proximity to the Communist world, and her advanced and stable economy and society, all made it natural that she should

eventually take her place in the security system built up by the United States in Asia and the Pacific. Its foundations were treaties with Australia, New Zealand and the Philippines (which had become independent in 1946). Others followed with Pakistan and Thailand; these were the Americans' only Asian allies other than Taiwan. Indonesia and (much more important) India remained aloof. These alliances reflected, in part, the new conditions of Pacific and Asian international relations after the British withdrawal from India. For a little longer there would still be British forces east of Suez, but Australia and New Zealand had discovered during the Second World War that the United Kingdom could not defend them and that the United States could. The fall of Singapore in 1942 had been decisive. Though British forces still sustained the Malaysians against the Indonesians in the 1950s and 1960s, their important colony at Hong Kong survived, they knew, only because it suited the Chinese that it should. On the other hand, there was no question of sorting out the complexities of the new Pacific by simply lining up states in the teams of the Cold War. The peace treaty with Japan itself caused great difficulty because United States policy saw Japan as a potential anti-Communist force while others – notably Australia and New Zealand – remembered 1941 and feared a revival of Japanese power.

ASIAN REJECTION OF WESTERN DOMINATION

American policy was not made only by ideology. None the less, it was long misled by what was believed to be the disaster of the Communist success in China and by Chinese patronage of revolutionaries as far away as Africa and South America. There had certainly been a transformation in China's

In 1954 SEATO was set up to maintain stability in Asia and the Pacific. A meeting was held in Washington on 8 November, 1954, to which representatives of the free nations were invited, together with Japanese prime minister Shigeru Yoshida (1878–1967), pictured here speaking at the meeting. Yoshida called upon the United States and other free nations to invest $4,000 million in Southeast Asia in order to reduce the risk of the region falling into Communist hands.

international position and it would go further. Yet the crucial fact was China's re-emergence as a power in her own right and in the end this did not reinforce the dualist, Cold War system but made nonsense of it. Though at first only within the former Chinese sphere, it was bound to bring about a big change in relative power relationships; the first sign of this was seen in Korea, where the United Nations armies were stopped and it became necessary to consider bombing China. But the rise of China was also of the most acute importance to the Soviet Union which from one pole of a bipolarized system became the corner of a triangle, as well as losing its unchallenged pre-eminence in the world revolutionary movement. And it was in relation to the Soviet Union, perhaps, that the wider significance of the Chinese Revolution most readily appeared. Overwhelmingly the most important though it might be, the Chinese Revolution was only the outstanding instance of a rejection of Western domination which was Asia-wide. Paradoxically, of course, that rejection in all Asian countries was most obviously expressed in forms, language and mythology borrowed from the West itself, whether they were those of industrial capitalism, nationalism or Marxism.

On 1 July, 1997, the British colony of Hong Kong was handed back to China: two scenes from the farewell celebrations are shown here. At the handover ceremony at the Hong Kong Convention Center (top), dignitaries from around the world were among the guests who watched the Chinese flag flying after the British Union Jack had been lowered. Later, a fireworks display lit up the harbour (bottom).

2 INHERITORS OF EMPIRE

THE SURVIVAL OF ISRAEL, the coming of the Cold War and a huge rise in the demand for oil revolutionized the politics of the Middle East after 1948. Israel focused Arab feeling more sharply than Great Britain had ever done. It enabled pan-Arabism to look plausible. On the injustice of the seizure of what were regarded as Arab lands, the plight of the Palestine refugees and the obligations of the great powers and the United Nations to act on their behalf, the Arab masses could brood bitterly and Arab rulers were able to agree as on nothing else.

ISRAEL AND THE ARAB STATES

AFTER THE DEFEAT of 1948–9, in spite of the new spirit of pan-Arabism, the Arab states were not for some time disposed again to commit their own forces openly. A formal

The Dome of the Rock in Jerusalem is an important Islamic shrine. In the period prior to the establishment of Israel, the struggle between the Jews and the Arabs was focused on the control of Jerusalem. Within the city, the Jewish and Arab quarters had long been mixed. In the war that followed the foundation of Israel, Jordanian forces occupied the old city and tried to blockade the Jews holding out in the new sector. The armistice of 1949 left Jerusalem divided, with an Israeli corridor to its sector of the city. From 1967, Israel occupied the former Jordanian sector. A unified Jerusalem is now the capital of Israel.

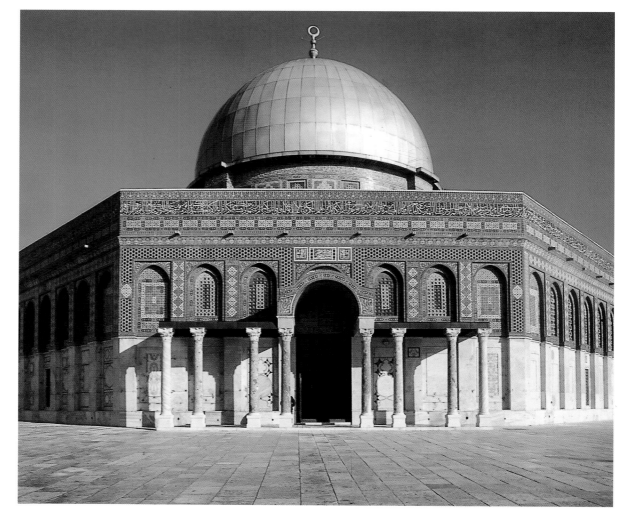

The post-Ottoman Near and Middle East

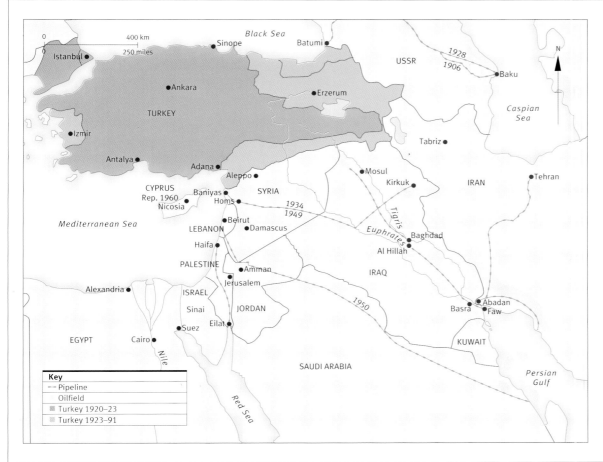

In many of the Muslim countries in the Near East foreign colonial powers have weakened and disappeared since the end of the Second World War, while Arab oil wealth has grown rapidly. It has been a tumultuous period in the region. The establishment of the state of Israel in 1948 was followed by the Arab–Israeli wars. In 1956 the Suez crisis took place. Soviet troops invaded Afghanistan in 1979 and fought in the civil war there until 1989, while civil war also raged in Lebanon from 1975 until 1989. Following the Iran–Iraq war of 1980–1989, Iraq's invasion of Kuwait in 1990 sparked off the Gulf War.

state of war persisted but a series of armistices established for Israel de facto borders with Jordan, Syria and Egypt which lasted until 1967. There were continuing border incidents in the early 1950s, and raids were carried out upon Israel from Egyptian and Syrian territory by bands of young guerrilla soldiers recruited from the refugee camps, but immigration, hard work and money from the United States steadily consolidated the new Israel. A siege psychology helped to stabilize Israel's politics; the prestige of the party which had brought about the very existence of the new state was scarcely troubled while the Jews transformed their new country. Within a few years they could show massive progress in bringing barren

land under cultivation and establishing industries. The gap between Israel's per capita income and that of the more populous among the Arab states steadily widened.

Here was another irritant for the Arabs. Foreign aid to their countries produced nothing like such dramatic change. Egypt, the most populous of them, faced particularly grave problems posed by high rates of population growth. While the oil-producing states were to benefit from growing revenue and a higher GDP, this often led to further strains and divisions. Contrasts between different Arab states, and between classes within them both deepened. Most of the oil-producing countries were ruled by small, wealthy, sometimes traditional and conservative, sometimes nationalist and westernized, élites, usually uninterested in the poverty-stricken peasants and slum-dwellers of more populous neighbours. The contrast was exploited by a new Arab political movement, founded during the war, the Ba'ath party. It attempted to synthesize Marxism and pan-Arabism, but the Syrian and Iraqi wings of the movement (it was always strongest in those two countries) had fallen out with one another almost from the start.

NASSER'S EGYPT

PAN-ARABISM HAD MUCH to overcome, for all the impulse to united action stemming from anti-Israeli and anti-Western feeling. The Hashemite kingdoms, the Arabian sheikdoms, and the Europeanized and urban states of North Africa and the Levant all had widely divergent interests and very different

Abdel Nasser (1918–1970) was one of the instigators of the Egyptian coup that overthrew King Farouk in 1952, and became president of the Revolutionary Council. Nasser was appointed head of government in 1954, a moment captured here, and president of Egypt in 1956. He played an important role in the Bandung Conference in 1955.

historical traditions. Some of them, like Iraq or Jordan, were artificial creations whose shape was dictated by the needs and wishes of European powers after 1918; some were social and political fossils. Even Arabic was in many places a common language only within the mosque (and not all Arabic-speakers were Muslims). Though Islam was a tie between many Arabs, it for a long time seemed little more; in 1950 few Muslims talked of it as a militant, aggressive faith. It was only the Israeli issue which provided a common enemy. Hopes were awoken among Arabs in many countries, nevertheless, by a revolution in Egypt from which there eventually emerged a young soldier, Gamal Abdel Nasser. For a time he seemed likely both to unite the Arab world against Israel and to open the way to social change. In 1954 he became the leader of the military junta which had overthrown the Egyptian monarchy two years previously. Egyptian nationalist feeling had for decades found its main focus and scapegoat in the British, still garrisoning the country, and now blamed for their part in allowing the establishment of Israel. The British government, for its part, did its best to cooperate with Arab rulers because of its fears of Russian influence in an area still thought crucial to British communications and oil supplies. The Middle East, ironically (given the motives which had taken the British there in the first place), did not seem to matter less after withdrawal from India.

EUROPEAN REACTIONS TO NASSER

The 1950s were a time of strong anti-Western currents elsewhere in the Arab world. In 1951 the king of Jordan had been assassinated; in order to survive, his successor had to make it clear that he had severed the old special tie with Great Britain. Further west, the French, who had been forced to recognize the complete independence of Morocco and Tunisia soon after the war, faced in 1954 the start of an Algerian national rebellion. It was to become a full-scale war; no French government could easily abandon a country where there were over a million settlers of European stock. Moreover oil had just been discovered in the Sahara. In such a context Nasser's rhetoric of social reform and nationalism had wide appeal. His anti-Israeli feelings were not in doubt and he quickly had to his credit the success of an agreement with Great Britain for the evacuation of the Suez base. The Americans, too, increasingly aware of Russian menace in the Middle East, looked on him for a while with favour as a spotless anti-colonialist and potential client.

He soon came to appeal to them less. The guerrilla raids on Israel from Egyptian territory (the "Gaza Strip", where the most important Palestinian refugee camps lay) provoked irritation in Washington. In 1950, the British, French and Americans had already said they would supply no arms to anyone in the area. When Nasser carried off an arms deal with Czechoslovakia on the security of the cotton crop and Egypt recognized Communist China, second thoughts about him hardened. By way of showing displeasure, an American and British offer to finance a cherished project of internal development, a high dam on the Nile, was withdrawn. As a riposte, Nasser seized the assets of the private company which owned and ran the Suez Canal, saying its profits should finance the dam; this touched an old nerve of British imperial sensibility. Instincts only half-disciplined by imperial withdrawal seemed for once to be coherent both with anti-Communism and with friendship towards more traditional Arab states whose rulers were beginning to look askance at Nasser as a

revolutionary radical. The British prime minister, too, was obsessed with a false analogy which led him to see Nasser as a new Hitler, to be checked before he embarked upon a career of successful aggression. As for the French, they were aggrieved by Nasser's support for the Algerian insurrection. Both nations formally protested over the canal's seizure and, in collusion with Israel, began to plan Nasser's overthrow.

The ancient statues at Abu Simbel in Egypt are relocated to make way for the Aswan High Dam. The dam, which was inaugurated in January 1971, impounds a vast reservoir called Lake Nasser and controls the annual Nile flood.

THE SUEZ CRISIS

IN OCTOBER 1956, the Israelis suddenly invaded Egypt to destroy, they announced, bases from which guerrillas harassed their

The Israeli offensive that began on the night of 29 October, 1956, took the Egyptians completely by surprise. On 1 November, Israeli troops continued to advance through Sinai and one day later they occupied Gaza. Here, jubilant Israeli troops pose with a captured Egyptian lorry in Gaza on 2 November.

settlements. The British and French governments at once said freedom of movement through the canal was in danger. They called for a cease-fire; when Nasser rejected this they launched (on Guy Fawkes' Day) first an air attack and then a seaborne assault on Egypt. Collusion with Israel was denied but the denial was preposterous. It was a lie, and, worse still, from the first incredible. Soon, the Americans were thoroughly alarmed; they feared advantage for the USSR in this renewal of imperialism. They used financial pressure to force a British acceptance of a cease-fire negotiated by the United Nations. The Anglo-French adventure ended in humiliation.

The Suez affair appeared to be (and was) a Western disaster, but in the long run its main importance was psychological. The British suffered most; it cost them much goodwill, particularly within the Common-wealth, and squandered confidence in the sincerity of their retreat from empire. It confirmed the Arabs' hatred of Israel; the suspicion that she was indissolubly linked to the West made them yet more receptive to Soviet blandishment. Nasser's prestige soared still higher. Some thought, too, that Suez had badly distracted the West at a crucial moment from Eastern Europe (where a revolution in Hungary against its Soviet satellite government had been crushed by the Russian army while the Western powers quarrelled with one another). Nevertheless, the essentials of the region's affairs were left by the crisis much as before, animated by a new wave of pan-Arab enthusiasm though they might be. Suez did not change the balance of the Cold War, or of the Middle East.

THE REPERCUSSIONS OF THE SUEZ CRISIS

In 1958 an attempt was made by Ba'ath sympathizers to unite Syria and Egypt in a United Arab Republic. It was briefly to bear fruit in 1961. The pro-Western government of the Lebanon was overthrown that year, and the monarchy of Iraq was swept aside by revolution. But differences between Arab countries soon reasserted themselves. The world watched curiously when American forces were summoned to the Lebanon and British to Jordan to help maintain their governments against pro-Nasser forces. Meanwhile, fighting went on sporadically on the Syrian-Israeli border, though the guerrillas were for a time held in check. From Suez to 1967 the most important development in the Arab world was none of these, but the Algerian revolution. The intransigence of the French settlers and the bitterness of many soldiers who felt they were asked to do an impossible job there nearly brought about a

From 1954, the National Liberation Front fought for the political independence of Algeria. On 12 March, 1962, a cease-fire was agreed: the republic of Algeria was recognized and guarantees for France's principal interests in the new state were made, along with agreements on future cooperation. Here, Prime Minister Muhammad Ben Bella gives a speech in the new Algerian National Assembly in 1962.

coup d'état in France itself. The government of General de Gaulle nevertheless opened secret negotiations with the Algerian rebels and in July 1962, after a referendum, France formally granted independence to a new Algeria. As Libya had emerged from United Nations trusteeship to independence in 1951, the entire North African coast outside the tiny Spanish enclaves was now clear of European supremacy. Yet external influences still bedevilled the history of the Arab lands as they had done ever since the Ottoman conquests centuries before, but now indirectly, through aid and diplomacy, as the United States and Russia sought to buy friends.

The United States laboured under a disadvantage: no American president or Congress could abandon Israel. The importance of Jews among American voters was too great, though President Eisenhower had been brave enough to face them down over Suez, even in an election year. In spite of America's clean hands therefore, Egyptian and Syrian policy continued to sound anti-American and prove irritating. The USSR, on the other hand, had dropped its early support of Israel as soon as it ceased to be a useful weapon with which to embarrass the British. Soviet policy now took a steady pro-Arab line and assiduously fanned Arab resentment over survivals of British imperialism in the Arab world. Marginally, too, the Russians earned a cheap bonus of Arab approval in the later 1960s by harassing their own Jews.

THE OIL FACTOR

The terms of the Middle Eastern problem were slowly changing because of oil. In the 1950s there were two important developments. One was a much greater rate of oil discovery than hitherto, particular on the southern shores of the Persian Gulf, in the small sheikdoms then still under British influence, and in Saudi Arabia. The second was a huge acceleration of energy consumption in Western countries, especially in the United States. The prime beneficiaries of the oil boom were Saudi Arabia, Libya, Kuwait and, some way behind, Iran and Iraq, the established major producers. This had two important consequences. Countries dependent upon Middle Eastern oil – the United States, Great Britain, Germany and, soon, Japan – had to give greater weight to Arab views in their diplomacy. It also meant big changes in the relative wealth and standing of Arab states. None of the three leading oil producers was either heavily populated or traditionally very weighty in international affairs.

THE SIX DAY WAR

The importance of the oil factor was still not very evident in the last Middle East crisis of the 1960s, which began when a much more extreme government took power in Syria with Russian support. The king of Jordan was threatened if he did not act in support of the Palestinian guerrillas (organized since 1964 as the Palestine Liberation Organization, or PLO). Jordanian forces therefore began to prepare to join in an attack on Israel with Egypt and Syria. But in 1967, provoked by an attempt to blockade their Red Sea port, the Israelis struck first. In a brilliant campaign they destroyed the Egyptian air force and army in Sinai and hurled back the Jordanians, winning in six days' fighting new borders on

An oil refinery in Jeddah, Saudi Arabia, is pictured. The sectors that turned the 1950s and 1960s into growth years in the industrialized nations (the car industry, steel and iron works, petrochemicals, electronics and construction) were dependent on oil. This meant that underdeveloped countries that had access to large oil reserves, particularly those in the Middle East, were suddenly able to influence international politics in a new way.

The Israeli defence minister, Moshe Dayan (left), waits in a bunker in the Golan Heights during the Six Day War. The war was a tactical victory for the Israelis. They managed to surround the Egyptian Third Army, which suffered such heavy losses that President Nasser temporarily resigned.

the Suez Canal, the Golan Heights, and the Jordan. For defence, these were far superior to their former boundaries and the Israelis announced that they would keep them. This was not all. Defeat had ensured the eclipse of the glamorous Nasser, the first plausible leader of pan-Arabism. He was left visibly dependent on Russian power (a Soviet naval squadron arrived at Alexandria as the Israeli advance-guards reached the Suez Canal), and on subsidies from the oil states. Both demanded more prudence from him, and that meant difficulties with the radical leaders of the Arab masses.

TENSIONS RISE OVER ISRAEL

The Six Day War of 1967 solved nothing. There were new waves of Palestinian refugees; by 1973 around 1,400,000 Palestinians were said to be dispersed in Arab countries, while a similar number remained in Israel and Israeli-occupied territory. When the

Israelis began to establish settlements in their newly won conquests, Arab resentment grew even stronger. Even if time, oil, and birth-rates seemed to be on the Arab side, not much else was clear. In the United Nations, a "Group of 77" supposedly non-aligned countries achieved the suspension of Israel (like South Africa) from certain international organizations and, perhaps more important, a unanimous resolution condemning the Israeli annexation of Jerusalem. Another called for Israel's withdrawal from Arab lands in exchange for recognition by her neighbours. Meanwhile, the PLO turned to terrorism outside the disputed lands to promote their cause. Like the Zionists of the 1890s, they had decided that the Western myth of nationality was the answer to their plight: a new state should be the expression of their nationhood, and like Jewish militants in the 1940s, they determined that assassination and indiscriminate murder would be their weapons. It was clear that in time there would be another war, and therefore a danger that, because of

the identification of American and Russian interests with opposing sides, a world war might suddenly blow up out of a local conflict, as in 1914.

The danger became imminent when Egypt and Syria attacked Israel on the Jewish holy day of Yom Kippur, in October 1973. The Israelis for the first time faced the prospect of military defeat by the greatly improved and Soviet-armed forces of their opponents. Yet once again they won, though only after the Russians were reported to have sent nuclear weapons to Egypt and the Americans had put their forces on the alert round the world. This grim background, like the possibility that the Israelis themselves might have nuclear weapons they would be prepared to use in extremity, was not fully discernible to the public at the time. More immediately obvious was the impact of the acts of other Arab states, led by Saudi Arabia. By announcing restrictions on oil supply to Europe, Japan and the United States they raised the possibility that the diplomatic support on which Israel had always been able to rely might not be available to her for ever: Israel might not always be able to count on guilt about the Holocaust, on sympathy and admiration for a civilized and liberal state in a backward region, and on the weight of Jewish votes in the United States. Though for the moment a UN force was put into Sinai to separate the Israelis and Egyptians, none of the region's fundamental problems had been solved.

THE OIL CRISIS

The impact of the new "oil diplomacy" had been immediate: oil prices shot up. A major change in world relationships had taken place. In the 1950s and most of the 1960s the United States and United Kingdom had been able to assure stable and cheap oil supplies through their informal influence on Iraq (down to 1963, when a Ba'ath régime seized power), the Gulf States and Saudi Arabia. In the 1970s this broke down under the strain, primarily, of the Israeli question. Overnight, economic problems which had gone grumbling along but were tolerable in the 1960s became acute. Dependence on oil imports played havoc with balance-of-payment problems. Even the United States was badly shaken, while Japan and Europe were soon showing signs of economic recession. There was even talk of a new world depression like that of the 1930s. The golden age of economic growth which had begun with postwar recovery came to an end, and poorer countries which depended on imported oil were the worst hit of all. Many of them were soon facing renewed price inflation and some a virtual obliteration of the surplus of earnings they needed in order to pay interest on their large debts to foreign creditors.

BLACK AFRICA

IN THE 1950s AND 1960s Africa underwent a dramatic decolonization which left some fragile new states behind. This was especially true south of the Sahara. In spite of the long European influence in the former Ottoman lands, direct European rule had always been

Elated Algerians celebrate the declaration of their country's independence from France on 3 July, 1962.

less radically innovative in the Islamic lands of the Atlantic and Mediterranean coasts than in black Africa, where the map and the legal status of most of the area was now transformed in two decades. France and Great Britain were the major colonial powers concerned in what was for a long time a surprisingly peaceful process (Italy had lost her last African territories in 1943). Only in Algeria did the making of a decolonialized Africa cost much bloodshed (though there was plenty to come in the post-colonial era, when African set about African). Though Portugal only gave in after a domestic revolution in 1974, colonialism elsewhere in Africa was replaced fairly peacefully well before that date. Both French and British politicians were anxious to retain, if they could, some sort of influence by ostentatiously benevolent interest in their former subjects; settlers, rather than imperial rulers, were the usual brake on withdrawal.

THE LEGACY OF COLONIALISM

Black Africa owes its present form in the main to decisions of nineteenth-century Europeans (just as much of the Middle East owes its framework to their successors in this century). New African "nations" were usually defined by the boundaries of former colonies. These boundaries often enclosed peoples of many languages, stocks and customs, over whom colonial administrations had provided little more than a formal unity. As Africa lacked the unifying influence of great indigenous civilizations such as those of Asia to offset the colonial fragmentation of the continent, imperial withdrawal from the continent was followed by its Balkanization. The doctrine of nationalism which appealed to the westernized African élites (Senegal, a Muslim country, had a president who was a writer of poetry in French and an expert on Goethe) confirmed a continent's fragmentation, often

Maputo, seen here, is the capital and main port of Mozambique, Africa. Now a one-party socialist republic, Mozambique achieved independence from Portugal in 1975 after a 13-year war. The country's exports include rice, rubber, jute and precious stones.

ignoring important realities which colonialism had contained or manipulated. The sometimes strident nationalism of new rulers was often a response to the dangers of centrifugal forces. West Africans combed the historical record – such as it was – of ancient Mali and Ghana, and East Africans brooded over the past which might be hidden in relics such as the ruins of Zimbabwe in order to forge national mythologies like those of earlier nation-makers in Europe as they strove to find unifying and rallying influences.

ECONOMIC PROBLEMS

Its new internal divisions were not Africa's only or its worst problems. In spite of the continent's great economic potential, the economic and social foundations for a prosperous future were shaky. Once again, the imperial legacy was significant. Colonial régimes in Africa left behind feebler cultural and economic infrastructures than in Asia. Rates of literacy were low and trained cadres of administrators and technical experts were small. Africa's important economic resources (especially in minerals) required for their exploitation skills, capital and marketing facilities which could only come in the near future from the world outside (and white South Africa long counted as "outside" to many black politicians). What was more, some African economies had only recently undergone disruption and diversion because of European needs and in European interests. During the war of 1939–45, agriculture in some of the British colonies had shifted towards the growing of cash crops on a large scale for export. Whether this was or was not in the long-term interests of peasants who had previously raised crops and livestock only for their own consumption is debatable, but what is certain is that the consequences

were rapid and profound. One was an inflow of cash in payment for produce the British and Americans needed. Some of this came through in higher wages, but the spread of a cash economy often had profound local effects. Unanticipated urban growth and regional development took place. Many African countries were thus tied to a particular pattern of development which was soon to show its vulnerabilities and limitations in the post-war world. Even the benevolent intentions of a programme like the British Colonial Development and Welfare Fund, or many international aid programmes, unintentionally helped to shackle African producers to a world market. In such circumstances, as populations rose more and more rapidly after 1960 and as disappointment with the reality of "freedom" from the colonial powers set in, discontent was inevitable.

Official trade agencies were established in Kenya after the Second World War, ending the monopoly of European businesses over the rural economy. Cotton picking in Watamu is shown here.

Decolonization in Africa and Asia

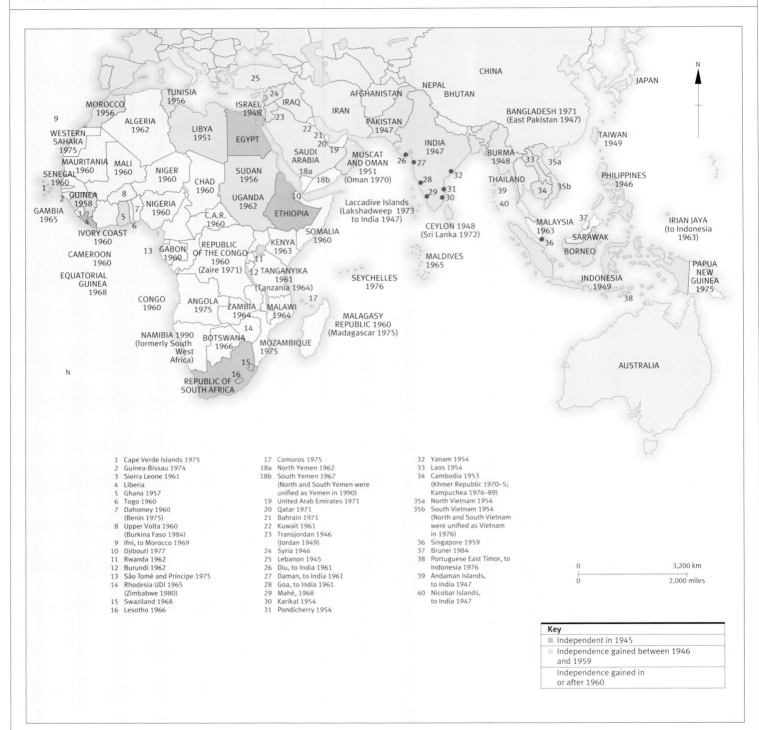

1	Cape Verde Islands 1975
2	Guinea-Bissau 1974
3	Sierra Leone 1961
4	Liberia
5	Ghana 1957
6	Togo 1960
7	Dahomey 1960 (Benin 1975)
8	Upper Volta 1960 (Burkina Faso 1984)
9	Ifni, to Morocco 1969
10	Djibouti 1977
11	Rwanda 1962
12	Burundi 1962
13	São Tomé and Príncipe 1975
14	Rhodesia UDI 1965 (Zimbabwe 1980)
15	Swaziland 1968
16	Lesotho 1966
17	Comoros 1975
18a	North Yemen 1962
18b	South Yemen 1967 (North and South Yemen were unified as Yemen in 1990)
19	United Arab Emirates 1971
20	Qatar 1971
21	Bahrain 1971
22	Kuwait 1961
23	Transjordan 1946 (Jordan 1949)
24	Syria 1946
25	Lebanon 1945
26	Diu, to India 1961
27	Daman, to India 1961
28	Goa, to India 1961
29	Mahé, 1968
30	Karikal 1954
31	Pondicherry 1954
32	Yanam 1954
33	Laos 1954
34	Cambodia 1953 (Khmer Republic 1970–5; Kampuchea 1976–89)
35a	North Vietnam 1954
35b	South Vietnam 1954 (North and South Vietnam were unified as Vietnam in 1976)
36	Singapore 1959
37	Brunei 1984
38	Portuguese East Timor, to Indonesia 1976
39	Andaman Islands, to India 1947
40	Nicobar Islands, to India 1947

0   3,200 km
0   2,000 miles

Key	
▪	Independent in 1945
	Independence gained between 1946 and 1959
	Independence gained in or after 1960

One of the crucial events in the modern world has been the access of various nations, mostly in the southern hemisphere, to political independence. As this map shows, decolonization effectively began in 1947 with the independence of India and Pakistan and ended around the mid-1970s. A number of countries have since changed their names or territorial boundaries, sometimes through unifications.

DECOLONIZATION

In spite of the difficulties experienced along the way, the process of decolonization in black Africa was hardly interrupted. In 1945 the only wholly independent countries in Africa other than Egypt had been Ethiopia and Liberia, though in reality and law the Union of South Africa was a self-governing dominion of the British Commonwealth and is therefore only formally excluded from this category (a slightly vaguer status also cloaked the virtual practical independence of the British colony of Southern Rhodesia). By 1961 (when South Africa became a fully independent republic and left the Commonwealth), twenty-four new African states had come into existence. There are now over fifty. Ten years later, Portugal was the only former colonial power still hanging on to black African possessions and by the end of 1975 they had gone, too. The Iberians who had led the European adventure of overseas dominion were almost the last to abandon it.

AFRICAN POLITICS

As Africans shook off colonialism, dangers quickly came to the surface. Ghana, in 1957, was the first ex-colonial new nation to emerge in sub-Saharan Africa. In the next 27 years twelve wars were to be fought in Africa and thirteen heads of state would be assassinated. There were two especially bad outbreaks of strife. In the former Belgian Congo an attempt by the mineral-rich region of Katanga to break away provoked a civil

K wame Nkrumah (1909–1972) was secretary of the 5th Pan-African Congress in 1945. He became the first prime minister of independent Ghana in 1957; in 1960 he declared Ghana a republic, and ruled as president until overthrown in 1966.

A s leader of the dominant KANU Party, Jomo Kenyatta (c.1891–1978) negotiated the terms of Kenya's independence from Great Britain in 1963 and became the first president of the republic in 1964. Along with other anti-colonial African leaders, he took part in the organization of the 5th Pan-African Congress in 1945.

The emperor of Ethiopia, Haile Selassie (1891–1975), is pictured during his coronation in 1930. Haile Selassie was deposed in 1974 by the military revolution, which proclaimed a Marxist popular republic.

days when a colonial system was in retreat.

In many of the new nations, the need, real or imaginary, to prevent disintegration, suppress open dissent and strengthen central authority, had led by the 1970s to one-party, authoritarian government or to the exercise of political authority by soldiers (it was not unlike the history of South America after the Wars of Liberation). Nor did the surviving régimes of an older independent Africa escape. Impatience with an *ancien régime* seemingly incapable of providing peaceful political and social change led in 1974 to revolution in Ethiopia. The setting aside of the "Lion of Judah" was almost incidentally the end of the oldest Christian monarchy in the world (and of a line of kings supposed in one version of the story to run back to the son of Solomon and the Queen of Sheba). A year later, the soldiers who had taken power seemed just as discredited as their predecessors. From similar changes elsewhere in Africa there sometimes emerged tyrant-like political leaders who reminded Europeans of earlier dictators, but this comparison may be misleading. Africanists have gently suggested that many of the "strong men" of the new nations can be seen as the inheritors of the mantle of pre-colonial African kingship, rather than in Western terms. Some were simply bandits, though.

AFRICAN ALLIANCES

Their own troubles did not diminish the frequent irritation with which many Africans reacted to the outside world. Some of the roots of this may lie very deep, in (for example) the mythological drama built on the old European slave trade, which Africans were encouraged to see as a supreme example of racial exploitation, or in the sense of political inferiority which lay near the surface in a

The emperor of Ethiopia, Haile Selassie (1891–1975), is pictured during his coronation in 1930. Haile Selassie was deposed in 1974 by the military revolution, which proclaimed a Marxist popular republic.

war in which rival Soviet and American influences quickly became entangled, while the United Nations strove to restore peace. Then, at the end of the 1960s, came a distressing civil war in Nigeria, hitherto one of the most stable and promising of the new African states, which again drew non-Africans to dabble in the blood-bath (one reason was that Nigeria had joined the ranks of the oil producers). In other countries, there were less bloody but still fierce struggles between factions, regions and tribes which distracted the small westernized élites of politicians and quickly led them to abandon democratic and liberal principles much talked of in the heady continent of relatively powerless states (some with populations of less than a million). In political and military terms, a disunited Africa could not expect to have much weight in international affairs. Attempts were therefore made to overcome the weakness which arose from division. An abortive attempt in 1958 to found a United States of Africa opened an era of alliances, partial unions, and essays in federation which had culminated in the emergence in 1963 of the Organization of African Unity (the OAU), largely thanks to the Ethiopian emperor, Haile Selassie.

Politically, the OAU had little success, though it concluded in 1975 a beneficial trade negotiation with Europe in defence of African producers. The very disappointment of much of the early political history of independent Africa directed thoughtful politicians towards cooperation in economic development, above all in relation to Europe, whose former colonial powers remained Africa's most important source of capital, skill and counsel. Unfortunately, the economic record of black Africa has been dreadful. Unsuitable schemes have led to agricultural decline. Political concern with urban voters, corruption and prestigious investment have played havoc

The Organization of African Unity

The newly independent African countries have tried to maintain the ideals and principles of Pan-Africanism not as a formula for a narrow, absolutist political federation, but rather as a continental union that expresses the fundamental identity of the independent African peoples.

This attempt to move towards unity and mutual cooperation crystallized with the establishment of the Organization of African Unity in May 1963, at the Conference of Heads of State and Government held in Addis Ababa (Ethiopia). Three factors led to the establishment of the OAU: the continuation of the pan-African ideal of unity; the radicalization of the fight for complete independence for all the countries on the African continent; and the harmonization of the different existing tendencies in those countries that were already independent.

The constitutional charter set out the objectives and principles that were to govern independent Africa, as well as the rights and obligations of the members. Some of the most outstanding objectives were to collaborate in improving living standards for the people of Africa, to defend the sovereignty, territorial integrity and independence of member states, and to favour international cooperation based on the United Nations Charter and the Universal Declaration of the Rights of Man. Its principles include non-interference in the internal affairs of the member countries; peaceful solutions to disputes through negotiation, mediation, conciliation or arbitration; and non-alignment with the major blocs.

Emperor Haile Selassie of Ethiopia (right) greets President Julius Nyerere of Tanzania as he arrives in Addis Ababa to attend the 10th anniversary of the OAU.

The term *apartheid* was first used in 1948 by the South African senator Hendrik Verwoerd, when he asserted the need to maintain white supremacy in South Africa. One of the apartheid laws, the Reservation of Separate Amenities Act, decreed that all public services were to be destined for the use of either whites or non-whites; this affected buildings, beaches, parks, public benches, buses and even, as this picture shows, public conveniences.

with commercial and industrial policy. Meanwhile, population inexorably rises, and famine has inexorably recurred. The onset of world economic recession after the 1973 oil revolution had a shattering effect on Africa, one worsened within a few years by the impact of repeated drought. In black Africa annual per capita growth in GDP has turned downward since 1960, and fell by 1.7 per cent from 1980 to 1985.

Political cynicism flourished against this background and the leaders of the independence era often seemed to lose their way. Yet they showed an almost total lack of self-criticism and often expressed their frustration in the encouragement of new resentments (sometimes exacerbated by external attempts to entangle Africans in the Cold War). These could be disappointing, too. Marxist revolution had little success. Paradoxically, it was only in Ethiopia, most feudally backward of independent African states, and the former Portuguese colonies, the least-developed former colonial territories, that formally

Marxist régimes took root. Former French and British colonies were hardly affected.

SOUTH AFRICA AND RHODESIA

SCAPEGOATS, INEVITABLY, were sought on whom Africa's problems could be blamed. Increasingly, but perhaps explicably, given the completeness and rapidity of decolonization in Africa and the geographical remoteness of much of it, they tended to be found at hand; resentments came to focus more on the racial division of black and white in Africa itself. This was flagrant in the most powerful of African states, the Union of South Africa.

THE APARTHEID SYSTEM

The Afrikaans-speaking Boers who by 1945 dominated South Africa cherished grievances against the British which went back to the

Great Trek, had been intensified by defeat in the Boer War and had then led to the progressive destruction of ties with the British Commonwealth after the First World War. This had been made easier by the concentration of voters of Anglo-Saxon origin in the provinces of Cape Town and Natal; the Boers were entrenched in the Transvaal and the major industrial areas as well as the rural hinterland. South Africa, it is true, entered the war in 1939 on the British side and supplied important forces to fight in it, but even then intransigent "Afrikaners", as they increasingly called themselves, supported a movement favouring cooperation with the Nazis. Its leader became prime minister in 1948, after defeating South Africa's senior statesman, Jan Smuts, in a general election. As the Afrikaners had steadily engrossed power inside the Union, and had built up their economic position in the industrial and financial sectors, the prospect of imposing a policy towards black Africans which diverged from their deep prejudices was soon inconceivable. The eventual result was the construction of a system of separation of the races: apartheid. It systematically embodied and reinforced the reduction of black Africans to the inferior status they occupied in Boer ideology. Its aim was to guarantee the position of the whites in a land where industrialism and market economies had done much to break down the regulation and distribution of the growing black population by the old tribal divisions.

SOUTHERN RHODESIA SECEDES FROM THE COMMONWEALTH

Apartheid had some appeal – on even less excusable grounds than the primitive superstitions or supposed economic necessities of the Afrikaners – to white people elsewhere in Africa. The only country where a similar balance of black and white population to that of South Africa and a similar concentration of wealth existed was Southern Rhodesia which, to the great embarrassment of the British government, seceded from the Commonwealth in 1965. The aim of the secessionists, it was feared, was to move towards a society more and more like South Africa's. The British government dithered and missed its chance. There was nothing that the black African states could immediately do about Rhodesia, and not much that the United Nations could do either, though "sanctions" were invoked in the form of an embargo on trade with the former colony; many black African states ignored them and the British government winked at the steps taken by major oil companies to ensure their product reached the rebels. In one of the most shameful episodes in the history of a feeble government, Great Britain's stock sank in the eyes of Africans who, understandably, did not see why a British government could not intervene

Pictured are two workers in a gold mine near Johannesburg in 1948. The gold industry, together with diamond mining, created most of South Africa's wealth. The country's economy grew at a tremendous rate from 1960 to 1970, with GDP increasing by 113 per cent, and the population by 34 per cent. This new wealth, however, was unevenly distributed among the population.

militarily to suppress a colonial rebellion as flagrant as that of 1776. Many British reflected that precisely that precedent made the outlook for intervention by a remote and militarily weak imperial sovereign look discouraging.

Though South Africa (the richest and strongest state in Africa, and growing richer and stronger all the time) seemed secure, she was, together with Rhodesia and the Portuguese colonies, the object of mounting black African anger as the 1970s began. The drawing of the racial battle lines was hardly offset by minor concessions to South Africa's black population and her growing economic ties with some black states. There was a danger, too, that outside powers might soon be involved. In 1975, after the Portuguese withdrawal from Angola, a Marxist régime took power there. When civil war followed, foreign Communist soldiers arrived to support the government, while South African support was soon given to rebels against it.

ZIMBABWE

The South African government soon showed it was taking thought. It sought to detach itself from the embarrassment of association with an unyielding independent Rhodesia (whose prospects had sharply worsened when Portuguese rule also came to an end in Mozambique and a guerrilla campaign was launched from it against her). The American government contemplated the outcome if Rhodesia collapsed at the hands of black nationalists depending on Communist support. It applied pressure to the South Africans, who, in turn, applied it to the Rhodesians. In September 1976 the Rhodesian prime minister sadly told his countrymen that they had to accept the principle of black majority rule. The last attempt to found an African country dominated by whites had failed. It was another landmark in the recession of European power. Yet the guerrilla war continued, worsening as black nationalists sought to

Thousands of refugees fled the Rhodesian war. These children were photographed in Zambia in 1977.

achieve unconditional surrender. At last, in 1980 Rhodesia briefly returned to British rule before re-emerging into independence, this time as the new nation of Zimbabwe, with a black prime minister.

GROWING OPPOSITION TO APARTHEID

The emergence of Zimbabwe left South Africa alone as the sole white-dominated state in the continent, the richest of its economies, and the focus of black (which, in this context, meant non-white) resentment the world around. Although the OAU had been split by civil war in Angola, African leaders could usually find common ground against South Africa. In 1974 the General Assembly of the UN forbade South Africa to attend its sessions because of *apartheid*, and in 1977 the UN Commission of Human Rights deftly sidestepped demands for the investigation of the horrors perpetrated by blacks against blacks in Uganda, while castigating South Africa (along with Israel and Chile) for its misdeeds. From Pretoria, the view north-wards looked more and more menacing. The arrival of Cuban troops in Angola showed a new power of strategic action against South Africa by the USSR. Both that former Portuguese colony and Mozambique also provided bases for South African dissidents who fanned unrest in the black townships and sustained urban terrorism in the 1980s.

CHANGE IN SOUTH AFRICA

International condemnation, the threat from the north and domestic unrest were no doubt among the factors which brought about changes in the position of the South African government. By the mid-1980s, the issue seemed to be no longer whether the more obnoxious features of apartheid should be

In April 1985 huge crowds attended the funerals in Vitenhage of victims of South Africa's escalating violence, in this instance the result of an uprising staged by members of the United Democratic Front against the white minority government. In this period, factional conflict was also devastating the black communities. By July, President Botha had declared a state of emergency in most of the country's cities.

dismantled, but whether black majority rule could be conceded by South African whites, and whether it could happen without armed conflict. A change was apparent when a new prime minister took office in 1978. To the dismay of many Afrikaners, Mr P.W. Botha began slowly to unroll a policy of concession. Before long, though, his initiative slowed; continuing signs of hostility to South Africa in the United Nations, urban terrorism at home, an increasingly dangerous and militarily demanding situation on the northern frontiers in Namibia (allocated to South Africa years before as a UN trusteeship territory), and increased distrust of Botha among his Afrikaner supporters (shown in elections), all led him back towards repression. His last gesture to relaxation was a new constitution in 1983 which provided representation for non-white South Africans in a way which outraged black political leaders by its inadequacy, and disgusted white

conservatives by conceding the principle of non-white representation at all.

Meanwhile, the pressure of what were called "sanctions" against South Africa by other countries was growing. In 1985 even the United States imposed them to a limited extent; by then, international confidence in the South African economy was falling, and the effects were showing at home. Straws before the wind of change in domestic opinion could be discerned in the decision of the Dutch Reformed Church that apartheid was at least a "mistake" and could not (as had been claimed) be justified by Scripture, and in growing division among Afrikaner politicians. It probably helped, too, that in spite of its deepening isolation, South African military action successfully mastered the border threats, though it was incapable of defeating the Angola government so long as Cuban forces remained there. In 1988 Namibia came to independence on terms

Nelson Mandela is pictured on the day of his inauguration as president of South Africa in May 1994, at a celebrity football match between Zambia and South Africa.

South Africa found satisfactory and peace was made with Angola.

NELSON MANDELA IS FREED

This was the background against which Mr Botha (president of the republic since 1984) reluctantly and grumpily stepped down in 1989 and Mr F.W. de Klerk succeeded him. He soon made it clear that the movement towards liberalization was to continue and would go much further than many thought possible, even if this did not mean the end of apartheid in all respects. Political protest and opposition were allowed much more freedom. Meetings and marches were permitted, imprisoned black Nationalist leaders were released. In 1990 the symbolic figure of Mr Nelson Mandela, leader of the African National Congress, emerged at last from jail. He was before long engaged in discussion with the government about what lay ahead. For all the intransigence of his language, there were hopeful signs of a new realism that the task of reassuring the white minority about a future under a black majority must be attempted. Just such signs, of course, prompted other black politicians to greater impatience.

By the end of 1990 Mr de Klerk had gone a long way. He had taken his followers further than Mr Mandela had taken his. He had even said he would rescind the land legislation which was the keystone of apartheid. In 1991, at last, the other apartheid laws were repealed. This offered grounds for maintained optimism. At the same time, doubts multiplied about the dangers of escalating violence, as demands were made for further concessions to black South Africans.

Nineteen ninety-three was a particularly violent year, with the security forces under growing pressure, yet before it ended the

South African parliament at last approved constitutional changes which promised to give the black population a real share in political power. It accepted a new interim constitution under which free elections were to be held the following year. This was a huge step by the responsible leaders, both black and white, and its fruits came in April 1994 when the choice of a new parliament was made without disorder in elections which secured a wide turnout of black voters. When the new parliament met, on 9 May, it chose Mr Mandela as the first president of a new South Africa. Whatever difficulties lay ahead – and there were many, notably in the unresolved disappointments of extremists black and white, and in the huge social and economic needs of the new state – this was by any standard one of the great positive political achievements of the century.

LATIN AMERICA

B Y 1900, SOME LATIN AMERICAN countries were beginning to settle down not only to stability but to prosperity. To the original colonial implantation of culture had been added the influence of nineteenth-century Europe, especially of France, to which Latin American élites had been drawn in the post-colonial period. Their upper classes were highly Europeanized and the modernity of

many of the continent's great cities reflected this, as their populations reflected recent European immigration which was swallowing the old colonial élites. As for the descendants of the aboriginal Americans, they were hardly to be taken into account. Their suppression had been so complete in one or two countries as to approach even their extinction.

LATIN AMERICA BEFORE 1914

Almost all Latin American states were primary producers, whether of agricultural or mineral resources. Although some were relatively highly urbanized, their manufacturing sectors were inconsiderable, and for a long time did not seem to be troubled by the social and political problems of nineteenth-century Europe. Capital had flowed into the continent, only briefly and occasionally checked by periodic financial disasters and disillusionments. The only social revolution in a Latin American state before 1914 (as opposed to countless changes in governmental personnel) overthrew the Mexican dictator Porfirio Díaz in 1911. It opened the way to nearly ten years' fighting and a million deaths, but the primary role in it was played by a middle class which felt excluded from the benefits of the régime, not by an industrial proletariat. Latin American countries did not display the class conflict of industrialized Europe in spite of large-scale nineteenth-century immigration, though in rural areas there was class conflict aplenty.

INSTABILITY BETWEEN THE WARS

Latin America's promising-looking societies survived the First World War prosperously. It brought important changes in their relations with Europe and North America. Before

The problem of the division of land was enormous in early 20th-century Mexico; figures have been put as high as 470,000 landowners and 14 million landless peasants. The 1910 insurrection against President Porfirio Díaz had the support of the revolutionary peasant leaders, such as Emiliano Zapata and Pancho Villa, pictured here with his brigade. Villa presented a programme of agricultural revolution based on granting land to the peasants.

Getulio Vargas, president of Brazil 1930–1945 and 1951–1954, arrives in Rio de Janeiro to watch a parade in December 1934. As the leader of the Liberal Alliance, Vargas had spearheaded opposition to Brazil's oligarchical republic and set himself up as spokesman for the burgeoning industrial middle classes. His régime represented the first attempt at popular government in Latin America.

1914, though she was the predominant political influence in the Caribbean, the United States did not yet exercise much economic weight in South America's affairs. In 1914 she supplied only seventeen per cent of all foreign investment south of the Rio Grande; Great Britain was far ahead of her. The liquidation of British holdings in the Great War changed this; by 1929 the United States was the largest source of investment in South America, providing about forty per cent of the continent's foreign capital. Then came the world economic crisis; 1929 was the doorway to a new and unpleasant era for the Latin American states, the true beginning of their twentieth century. Many defaulted on their payments to foreign investors. It became almost impossible to borrow further capital abroad. The collapse of prosperity led to growing nationalist assertiveness, sometimes against other Latin American states, sometimes against the North Americans and Europeans; foreign oil companies were expropriated in Mexico and Bolivia. The traditional Europeanized oligarchies were compromised by their failure to meet the problems posed by falling national incomes. From 1930 onwards there were military coups in every country except Mexico.

INDUSTRIALIZATION

Nineteen thirty-nine again brought prosperity as commodity prices rose because of wartime demand (in 1950 the Korean War prolonged this trend). In spite of the notorious admiration of Argentina's rulers for Nazi Germany, most of the republics were sympathetic to the Allies, who courted them; most joined the United Nations' side before the war ended, and one, Brazil, sent a small expeditionary force to Europe, a striking gesture. The most important effects of the war on Latin America, though, were economic. One, of

Juan Domingo Perón, who was president of Argentina from 1946 to 1955 and 1973 to 1974, salutes the crowds in Buenos Aires in 1952, accompanied by his wife, Eva. Perón had been appointed minister of employment after the 1943 *coup d'état*. His 1946 election programme included agrarian reform and autarky.

great significance, was that the old dependence on the United States and Europe for manufactured goods now became apparent in shortages. An intensive drive to industrialize gathered speed in several countries. On the urban workforces which industrialization built up was founded a new form of political power which entered the lists as a competitor with the military and the traditional élites in the post-war era. Authoritarian, semi-fascist, but popular mass movements brought to power a new kind of strong man. Perón in Argentina was the most famous, but Colombia in 1953 and Venezuela in 1954 threw up similar rulers. Communism had no such conspicuous success among the masses.

COLD WAR ANXIETIES

A significant change also came about (though not as a result of war) in the way the United States used its preponderant power in the Caribbean. Twenty times in the first twenty years of the century American armed forces had intervened directly in neighbouring republics, twice going so far as to establish protectorates. Between 1920 and 1939 there were only two such interventions, in Honduras in 1924 and Nicaragua two years later. Indirect pressure also declined. In large measure this was a sensible recognition of changed circumstances. There was nothing to be got by direct intervention in the 1930s and President Roosevelt made a virtue of this by proclaiming a "Good Neighbour" policy

Post-war Latin America

Latin America has long been plagued by serious intermittent economic difficulties, agricultural problems, illiteracy and accelerated demographic growth, which have influenced politics, encouraging populism and demagoguery. For most Latin American nations, independence from colonial rule did not bring economic independence: their dependence on outsiders continues to grow and to influence domestic politics. The boxes on this map show the amount of economic aid (in millions of US dollars) received by Latin American countries between 1961 and 1964.

Women from a village near Riobambas in the Ecuadorean Andes carry water from a pump funded by American aid back to their mountain homes in 1961.

which stressed non-intervention by all American states in one another's affairs. Yet after 1950 there was another change. While American policy was dominated by European concerns in the early phase of the Cold War, after Korea it began slowly to look southwards again. Washington had not been unduly alarmed by manifestations of Latin American nationalism which tended to find a scapegoat in American policy, but became increasingly concerned lest the hemisphere provide a lodgement for Russian influence.

The Cold War had come to it, and there followed greater selectivity in giving support to Latin American governments and, at times, to covert operations: for example, to the overthrow in 1954 of a government in Guatemala which had Communist support.

At the same time United States policy-makers were anxious that the footholds provided for Communism by poverty and discontent should be removed. They provided more economic aid (Latin America had only a tiny fraction of what went to Europe and Asia in the 1950s but much more in the next decade) and applauded governments which said they sought social reform. Unfortunately, whenever the programmes of such governments moved towards the eradication of American control of capital by nationalization, American policy tended to veer away again, demanding compensation on such a scale as to make reform very difficult. On the whole, therefore, while it might deplore the excesses of an individual authoritarian régime, such as that of Cuba before 1958, the American government tended to find itself, as in Asia, supporting conservative interests in Latin America. This was not invariably so; some governments acted effectively, notably Bolivia, which carried out land reform in 1952. But it remained true that, as for most of the previous century, the worst-off Latin Americans had virtually no hearing from either populist or conservative rulers, in that both listened only to the towns – the worst-off, of course, were the peasants, for the most part American Indians by origin.

REVOLUTION IN CUBA

For all the Americans' nervousness the revolutionary change in Latin America was small. This was one of the lessons of the only victorious revolution, that in Cuba, of which so much was hoped and feared at the time. That country was in a number of respects very exceptional. Its island position in the Caribbean, within a relatively short distance of the United States, gave it special significance. The approaches to the Canal Zone had often been shown to have even more importance in American strategical thinking than Suez in the British. Secondly, Cuba had been especially badly hit in the depression; it was virtually dependent on one crop, sugar, and that crop had only one outlet, the United States. This economic tie, moreover, was only one of several which gave Cuba a closer and more irksome "special relationship" with the United States than had any other Latin American state. There were historic connexions which went back to before 1898 and the winning of independence from Spain. Until 1934 the Cuban constitution had included special provisions restricting Cuba's diplomatic freedom. The Americans kept a naval base on the island (as they still do). There was heavy American investment in urban property and utilities, and Cuba's poverty and low prices made it an attractive holiday resort for Americans. All in all, it should not have been surprising that Cuba produced, as it did, a strongly anti-American nationalist movement with much popular support.

FIDEL CASTRO

The United States was seen as the real power behind the conservative post-war Cuban régime. Under the dictator Batista who came to power in 1952 this in fact ceased to be so; the State Department disapproved of him and cut off help to him in 1957. By the time this happened a young nationalist lawyer, Fidel Castro, had already begun a guerrilla campaign against his government. In two years he was successful. In 1959, as prime minister of

a new, revolutionary, Cuba, he described his régime as "humanistic" and, specifically, not communist.

Castro's original aims are still not known. Perhaps he was himself not clear what he thought. From the start he worked with a wide spectrum of people who wanted to overthrow Batista, from liberals to Marxists. This helped to reassure the United States, which patronized him as a Caribbean Sukarno; American public opinion idolized him as a romantic figure and beards became fashionable among American radicals. The relationship quickly soured once Castro turned to interference with American business interests, starting with agrarian reform and the nationalization of sugar concerns. He also denounced publicly those Americanized elements in Cuban society which had supported the old régime. Anti-Americanism was a logical means – perhaps the only one – open to Castro for uniting Cubans behind the revolution. Soon the United States broke off diplomatic relations with Cuba and began to bring to bear other kinds of pressure as well. The American government became convinced that the island was likely to fall into the hands of the Communists upon whom Castro

Fidel Castro (b.1927) takes part in a press conference in Havana in January 1959. In April that year, during his trip to the United States, Castro announced, "We are not communists". A few weeks later, Cuban political parties were repressed, the elections were delayed and the régime appeared to show communist leanings. Some historians claim that it was pressure from the United States that brought about this apparent change of political direction.

increasingly relied. It did not help when the Soviet leader Khrushchev warned the United States of the danger of retaliation from Soviet rockets if it acted militarily against Cuba and declared the Monroe doctrine dead; the State Department quickly announced that reports of its demise were greatly exaggerated. Finally the American government decided to promote his overthrow by force.

THE BAY OF PIGS OPERATION

It was agreed that Castro should be overthrown by Cuban exiles. When the presidency changed hands in 1961 Kennedy inherited this policy. Exiles were already training with American support in Guatemala, and diplomatic relations with Cuba had been broken off. He had not initiated it, but he was neither cautious nor thoughtful enough to impede it. This was the more regrettable because there was much else which promised well in the new president's attitude to Latin America, where it had been obvious for some time that the United States

needed to cultivate goodwill. As it was, the possibilities of a more positive approach were almost at once blown to pieces by the fiasco known as the "Bay of Pigs" operation, when an expedition of Cuban exiles supported by American money and arms came to a miserable end in April 1961. Castro now turned in earnest towards Russia, and at the end of the year declared himself a Marxist-Leninist.

A new and much more explicit phase of the Cold War thus began in the western hemisphere, and began badly for the United States. The American initiative incurred disapproval everywhere because it was an attack on a popular, solidly based régime. Henceforth, Cuba was a revolutionary magnet in Latin America. Castro's torturers replaced Batista's and his government pressed forward with policies which, together with American pressure, badly damaged the economy, but embodied egalitarianism and social reform (in the 1970s, Cuba claimed to have the lowest child mortality rates in Latin America).

THE CUBAN MISSILE CRISIS

Almost incidentally and as a by-product of the Cuban revolution there soon took place the most serious confrontation of the whole Cold War and perhaps its turning-point. It is not yet known why or how the Soviet government decided to install in Cuba missiles capable of reaching anywhere in the United States and thus roughly to double the number of American bases or cities which were potential targets. Nor is it known whether the initiative came from Havana or Moscow. Though Castro asked the USSR for arms, it seems likeliest that it was the second. But whatever the circumstances, American photographic reconnaissance confirmed in October 1962 that the Russians were building missile sites in Cuba. President Kennedy waited until

US president Kennedy and Soviet premier Khrushchev meet in Vienna, Austria, in June 1961 to discuss tensions over Berlin and differing views on Cuba.

this could be shown to be incontrovertible and then announced that the United States navy would stop any ship delivering further missiles to Cuba and that those already in Cuba would have to be withdrawn. One Lebanese ship was boarded and searched in the days that followed; Russian ships were only observed. The American nuclear striking force was prepared for war. After a few days and some exchanges of personal letters between Kennedy and Khrushchev, the latter agreed that the missiles should be removed.

THE FAILURE OF THE ALLIANCE FOR PROGRESS

This crisis by far transcended the history of the hemisphere, and its repercussions for the rest of the world are best discussed elsewhere. So far as Latin American history is concerned, though the United States promised not to invade Cuba, it went on trying to isolate it as much as possible from its neighbours. Unsurprisingly, the appeal of Cuba's revolution nevertheless seemed for a while to gain ground among the young of other Latin American countries. This did not make their governments more sympathetic towards Castro, especially when he began to present Cuba as a revolutionary centre for the rest of the continent. In the event, as an unsuccessful attempt in Bolivia showed, revolution was not likely to prove easy. Cuban circumstances had been very atypical. The hopes entertained of mounting a peasant rebellion elsewhere proved illusory. Local communists, indeed, appear to have deplored Castro's efforts. While there were in some places plenty of materials about for revolution they turned out to be urban rather than rural and it was in the major cities that guerrilla movements were within a few years taking the headlines. Though spectacular and dangerous, it is not

LAUNCH POSITION

MISSILE-READY TENTS

MISSILE ERECTORS

clear that these movements enjoyed wide popular support, though the brutalities practised in dealing with them alienated middle-class support from authoritarian governments in some countries. Anti-Americanism continued to run high. Kennedy's hopes for a new American initiative, based on social reform, an "Alliance for Progress" as he termed it, made no headway against the animosity aroused by American treatment of Cuba. His successor as president, Johnson, did no better, perhaps because he was less interested in Latin America than in domestic reform and tended to leave hemisphere policy to fellow-Texans with business interests there. The initiative was never recaptured after the initial flagging of the Alliance. Worse still, it was overtaken in 1965 by fresh evidence of the old Adam of intervention, this time in the Dominican Republic, where, four years before, American help had assisted the overthrow and assassination of a corrupt and tyrannical dictator and his replacement by a reforming democratic government. When this was pushed aside by soldiers acting in defence of the privileged who felt threatened by

Pictures taken by the CIA in 1962 of missile launch pads in Cuba, such as these to the east of San Cristóbal, astounded and alarmed the US government. Close study of this image revealed between 16 and 32 missiles which could be made ready for action in less than a week.

support while the Communist threat seemed to endure. Chile nationalized the largest American copper company, the Bolivians took over oil concerns and the Peruvians American-owned plantations. In 1969 there was a historic meeting of Latin American governments at which no United States representative was present and *Yanqui* behaviour was explicitly and implicitly condemned. A tour undertaken by a representative of the president of the United States that year led to protest, riots, the blowing up of American property and requests to stay away from some countries. It was rather like the end of the previous decade, when a "goodwill" tour by Eisenhower's vice-president ended in him being mobbed and spat upon. All in all, it looked by 1970 as if Latin American nationalism was entering a new and vigorous

The policy adopted by Havana after the Bay of Pigs affair became clear when, in a visit to Moscow, the guerrilla leader Che Guevara (1928–1967), who had become a minister in Castro's government, requested more aid from the Soviet Union. The aid sent by Moscow whipped up American public opinion against Cuba. It also enraged anti-Castro Cubans living in the United States, pictured here demonstrating near the Soviet embassy in New York in October 1962.

reform, the Americans cut off aid; it looked as if, after all, the Alliance for Progress might be used discriminately. But aid was restored – as it was to other right-wing régimes – when Johnson came to power. A rebellion against the soldiers in 1965 resulted in the arrival of 20,000 American troops to put it down.

ANTI-AMERICANISM

By the end of the 1960s the Alliance had virtually been forgotten, in part because of the persistent fears of Communism which led American policy to put its weight behind conservatives, in part because the United States had plenty of more pressing problems elsewhere. One result was a new wave of attacks on American property by governments which did not have to fear the loss of American

The denunciation of exploitation

"Look at the background: unreturned value, that is to say, that did not return to Chile in the great copper mines (...). Between 1930 and 1969, $3,700 million have crossed the borders of our country, which have gone to increase the strength of the companies that, on an international scale, control copper fields across the five continents. In 1969, $166 million did not return. I must stress that $3,700 million comprises 40 per cent of Chile's total wealth, of the effort accumulated over 400 years by the Chilean people. Forty per cent of that wealth has left the country from 1930 to 1969 and this fact cannot be forgotten. Chile also knows that altogether, in roughly the same period, as well as through copper, something like $9,600 million has vanished through iron, saltpetre, electricity and telephones, which represents the total value of Chile's wealth (...) ."

An extract from a speech given by the newly elected president of Chile, Salvador Allende, on 21 December, 1970.

period. If Cuba-inspired guerrillas had ever presented a danger, they appeared to do so no longer. Once the spur of an internal fear was gone there was little reason for governments not to try to capitalize on anti-American feeling.

LATIN AMERICA UNDER STRAIN

It was clear that the real problems of Latin America were not being met. The 1970s, and still more, the 1980s revealed chronic economic troubles and, by 1985 it was reasonable to speak of an apparently insoluble crisis. There were several sources for this. For all its rapid industrialization, the continent was threatened by appalling population growth. The hundred or so million Latin Americans and Caribbean islanders of 1950 will probably have become five hundred millions by the year 2000. This huge rate of growth began to be obvious just as the difficulties of the Latin American economies were again beginning to show their intractability. The aid programme of the Alliance for Progress patently failed to cope with them, and failure spawned quarrels over the use of American funds. Social divisions remained menacing. Even the most advanced Latin American countries displayed vast discrepancies of wealth and education. Constitutional and democratic process, where they existed, seemed increasingly impotent to confront such problems. In the 1960s and 1970s, Peru, Bolivia, Brazil, Argentina and Paraguay all underwent prolonged authoritarian rule by soldiers and some of the upholders of those régimes undoubtedly believed that only authoritarianism could bring about changes of which civilian government had proved incapable.

Latin Americans' problems were vividly brought to the notice of the world not only by reports of torture and violent repression from countries like Argentina, Brazil and Uruguay,

Salvador Allende (1908–1973) became president of Chile in 1970, and immediately faced a critical situation: the country had a huge budget deficit and an enormous external debt. A military coup, led by General Augusto Pinochet, overthrew Allende's socialist government in September 1973. Allende, pictured here just before his death, was killed during the fight for control of the presidential palace.

all once regarded as civilized and constitutional states, but when Chile, a country with a more continuous history of constitutional democracy than other Latin American states, underwent a military coup which overthrew in 1973 a government many Chileans believed to be under the control of Communists. The counter-revolutionary movement had approval and probably support from the United States, but many Chileans acquiesced because they had been frightened by the revolutionary tendencies of the displaced elected régime. There followed the installation of a very authoritarian government. It long seemed unable to extract the country from economic disaster, though in the end it rebuilt the economy and even, in the late 1980s, began to look as if it might be able to liberalize itself.

ECONOMIC AND CULTURAL PROBLEMS

It was on a troubled and distracted continent that there fell, to cap its troubles, the oil crisis of the 1970s which finally sent the foreign debt problems of its oil-importing countries out of control. By 1990, most orthodox economic remedies had been tried, in one country or another, but had proved unworkable or unenforceable in dealing with runaway inflation, interest charges on extended debt, the distortion in resource allocation arising from bad government in the past, and simple administrative and cultural inadequacy for the support of good fiscal policies. It remains impossible to guess how the complex and consequent economic crisis can be surmounted. While it is not, Latin America remains an explosive, disturbed continent of nations less and less like one another, for all their shared roots, except in their distress. Most Latin Americans are now poorer, if per capita income is the measure, than ten years ago. Even culture is still a divisive force. To the layers laid down by Indian, slave, colonial and post-colonial experiences, all of which were reflected strongly in differences of economic level, have now been added the differences brought by the arrival in the 1950s and 1960s of the assumptions of developed, high-technology societies, whose benefits are available to the better-off but not to the poor who observe them. Just as in Asia, though the world's imagination has hardly begun to grasp it, the strains of the impact of modern civilization on a historically deep-rooted society are now more obvious than ever before. Latin America has been undergoing some of them since the sixteenth century, but they are now expressed additionally through the terrorism displayed by radical revolutionaries and reactionary soldiers alike, and they continue to undermine civilized and constitutional standards already achieved.

In this view of Rio de Janeiro, the poverty of the well-established shanty town in the foreground contrasts sharply with the modern skyscrapers beyond, home to office suites and wealthy Brazilian families.

3 CRUMBLING CERTAINTIES

COMECON, founded in 1949, recognized the existence of nationalist paths to socialism and sought to promote economic cooperation among the countries of the Eastern bloc. Here Nikita Khrushchev (centre), Soviet premier from 1958 to 1964, and the East German politician Walter Ulbricht are applauded by crowds in East Berlin in 1958.

IN THE MIDDLE OF THE 1970s, the two giants still dominated the world as they had done since 1945, and they still often talked as if they divided it, too, into adherents or enemies. But there had been changes in the way they were regarded. The United States was widely believed to have lost its once overwhelming military preponderance over the Soviet Union and those easily frightened by signs of instability wondered what would happen if there was to be a new Cuban crisis. Others found reassurance in such a shift: perhaps a more even balance would make such a crisis unlikely. The superpowers had to live in a changing environment, moreover. The

two once more-or-less-disciplined blocs surrounded by small fry trying to escape from being swallowed by them were showing signs of strain. New quarrels were beginning to cut across old ideological divisions. More interesting still, there were signs that new aspirants to the role of superpower might be emerging. Some people had even begun to talk about an era of détente.

SUPERPOWER DIFFICULTIES

ONCE AGAIN, THE ROOTS OF CHANGE go back some way; there are no sharp dividing lines between phases even if things looked more frozen than ever after the Cuba crisis. The death of Stalin, for instance, could hardly have been without effect, though it brought no obvious immediate change in Russian policy, and even more difficulty in interpreting it. The subsequent changes of personnel, whose outcome after nearly two years was the emergence of Nikita Khrushchev in a directing role, and the retirement in 1956 of Molotov, Stalin's old henchman and veteran of Cold War diplomacy, from his post as foreign minister, were followed, too, by a sensational speech made by Khrushchev at a secret session of the twentieth congress of the Soviet Communist Party. In it he denounced the misdeeds of the Stalin era and declared "coexistence" the goal of Russian foreign policy. Given announcements of Soviet reductions in armaments it might be said that 1956 had already seemed a promising year for international change for the better, until the atmosphere was fouled by the Suez

Hungarian freedom fighters dismantle a statue of Stalin a few days after the Soviet invasion of 4 November, 1956. Imre Nagy (1895–1958), the Hungarian premier who opposed the Russians, was deposed, later to be executed, and a new Communist government was set up.

invasion and a contemporaneous revolution in Hungary. The first led to Soviet threats to Great Britain and France; the Russians were not going to risk Arab goodwill by failing to support Egypt openly. The second event operated against a deeper background, for ever since 1948 Soviet policy had been almost morbidly sensitive to signs of deviation or dissatisfaction among its satellites. In that year, Soviet advisers had been recalled from Yugoslavia, which was expelled from the Cominform. Her treaties with Russia and other Communist states were denounced by them and there followed five years of vitriolic attacks on "Titoism" (though, in the end, the Russians were to climb down and ask to reopen diplomatic relations).

REVOLUTION IN HUNGARY

Yugoslavia's damaging and embarrassing survival as a socialist state outside the Warsaw Pact left Russia sensitive to any tremor in the eastern camp. Anti-Soviet riots in East Berlin in 1953 and in Poland in the summer of 1956 had seemed to show that nationalism was still stronger than Communism. It was against this background that disturbances in Budapest in October 1956

Time chart (1950–1984)

	1950–1952 Schuman Plan and the formation of the ECSC	1963 J.F. Kennedy assassinated	1973 Treaty signed between the United States and North Vietnam to end the war	1979 Iranian revolution Saddam Hussein becomes president of Iraq	1982 Falklands War
1950				1980	
	1956 Soviet invasion of Hungary	1968 Martin Luther King assassinated Soviet invasion of Czechoslovakia		1976 Mao Tse-tung dies	1984 Indira Gandhi assassinated

A nti-Soviet demonstrators protest in the streets of East Berlin on 17 June, 1953. The régime adopted urgent measures to improve living conditions, but refused to make any political reforms.

grew into a nationwide movement which led to the withdrawal of Russian forces from the city, a new Hungarian government and a promise of free elections and the end of one-party rule. Unfortunately, the new régime soon went further, withdrawing from the Warsaw Pact, declaring Hungary's neutrality, and asking the United Nations to take up the Hungarian question. At this, the Russian army returned. The Hungarian revolution was crushed. The UN General Assembly twice condemned the intervention, and the episode hardened attitudes on both sides. The Russians were once more made aware of how little they were liked by the peoples of Eastern Europe, and therefore became even more distrustful of Western talk of "liberating" them. Western Europe was once again reminded of the real face of Soviet power, and sought to consolidate itself further.

Seeing danger in a rearmed West Germany, the Russians were anxious to strengthen their satellite, the German Democratic Republic. The continued existence of West Berlin inside its territory was a grave weakness. The city's frontiers were open and easily crossed. Its prosperity and freedom drew more and more East Germans – especially skilled workers – to the West. In 1958, this led the Russians to denounce the arrangements under which Berlin had been run since 1948; they said they would hand over their sector to the GDR if better ones could not be found. In August 1961, after some two years of drawn-out diplomacy, the East Germans suddenly erected a wall to cut off the Soviet sector of Berlin from the Western. They felt driven to do this by a huge increase in the outflow of refugees as the atmosphere of crisis over Berlin had deepened; 140,000 crossed in 1959, 200,000 in 1960 and more than 100,000 in the first six months of 1961. The new wall raised tension in the short run, but probably lowered it in the long. The GDR had succeeded in stopping emigration and Khrushchev quietly dropped his more extreme demands when it was clear that the United States was not prepared to give way over the legal status of Berlin even at the risk of war.

CONFRONTATION OVER CUBA

Substantially, this rhythm of mounting tension followed by détente was repeated the following year over Cuba, although the risk was then far greater. The allies of the United States were not so directly interested as they had been over a possible change in the German settlement, nor did the Russians seem to pay much attention to Cuba's interests. In a virtually "pure" confrontation of the superpowers the Soviet Union appeared to have been forced to give way. While avoiding action or language which might have been dangerously provocative, and while leaving a simple route of retreat open to his opponent by confining his demands to essentials, President Kennedy none the less made no apparent concessions, though, quietly, the

In August 1961 the Berlin Wall was erected along the demarcation line between the two sectors of the city, ending the exodus of thousands of East Germans. Here, another concrete slab is placed atop the wall in 1964.

withdrawal of American missiles from Turkey followed after a little while. Immediately, Khrushchev had to be satisfied with an undertaking that the United States would not invade Cuba.

It is difficult to believe that this was not a major turning-point. The prospect of nuclear war as the ultimate price of geographical extension of the Cold War had been faced and found unacceptable. The subsequent setting-up of direct telephone communication between the heads of the two states – the "hot line" – recognized that the danger of conflict through misunderstanding made necessary some more intimate connexion than the ordinary channels of diplomacy. It was also clear that in spite of Soviet boasting to the contrary, American preponderance in weapons was as great as ever. The new weapon which mattered for purposes of direct conflict between the two superpowers was the inter-

In 1962 several conferences on disarmament were held in Geneva, attended by representatives from the United States and the USSR. The talks mainly centred on the importance of restricting the number of countries able to stock nuclear weapons and preventing costly arms escalation. However, even as the talks progressed, multiple-head missiles and ABMs (anti-ballistic missiles) were being developed.

continental rocket missile; at the end of 1962 the Americans had a superiority in this weapon of more than six to one over the Russians, who set to work to reduce this disparity. The choice was made of rockets before butter and once again the Soviet consumer was to bear the burden. Meanwhile, the Cuban confrontation had probably helped to achieve the first agreement between Great Britain, the United States and the Soviet Union on the restriction of testing nuclear weapons in space, the atmosphere or under water. Disarmament would still be pursued without success for many years, but this was the first positive outcome of any negotiations about nuclear weapons.

KHRUSHCHEV FALLS

In 1964 Khrushchev was removed from office. As head of both government and party since 1958 it seems likely that his personal contribution to Soviet development had been to provide a great shaking-up. This brought qualified "de-Stalinization", a huge failure over agriculture, and a change in the emphasis of the armed services (towards the strategic rocket services which became their élite arm). Khrushchev had himself undertaken initiatives in foreign policy besides the disastrous Cuban adventure, and they may have been the fundamental cause of the decision to remove him. Yet though he was set aside with the connivance of the army by colleagues whom he had offended and alarmed, he was not killed, sent to prison or even to run a power-station in Mongolia. Evidently the Soviet Union was improving its techniques of political change. The contrast with earlier Soviet politics was striking and the nature of the régime such that people accounted this progress. Soviet society had relaxed a little after Stalin's death. The speech at the Twentieth Congress could not be unsaid, even if much of it was aimed at

Pictured during a reception in Moscow in 1962 are, from left to right: the Russian cosmonaut Yuri Gagarin, the Soviet premier Nikita Khrushchev, the Indonesian president Achmed Sukarno, and Leonid Brezhnev, who would replace Khrushchev two years later.

diverting criticism from those who (like Khrushchev himself) had been participants in the crimes of which Stalin was accused. (Symbolically, Stalin's body had been removed from Lenin's tomb, the national shrine.) In the next few years there was what some called a "thaw". Marginally greater freedom of expression was allowed to writers and artists, while the régime appeared briefly to be a little more concerned about its appearance in the eyes of the world over such matters as its treatment of Jews. But this was personal and sporadic: liberalization depended on who had Khrushchev's ear. It seems clear only that after Stalin's death, particularly during the era of Khrushchev's ascendancy, the party had re-emerged as a much more independent factor in Russian life. The authoritarian nature of the Russian government, though, seemed unchanged – which is what might have been expected.

DEFICIENCIES AND EFFICIENCIES IN THE SOVIET ECONOMY

Soviet authoritarianism makes it now seem odd that some came to think that the United States and Soviet Russia were growing more and more alike, and that this would help to make Russian policy less menacing. This theory of "convergence" gave a distorted emphasis to an undoubted truth: the Soviet Union was a developed economy. In the 1960s some still thought socialism a plausible road to modernization because of that. It was often overlooked that the Soviet economy was also inefficient and distorted. Soviet industrial growth, though faster than that of the United States at least in the 1950s, had long been overwhelmingly a matter of heavy manufacture. The private consumer in the Soviet Union remained poor by comparison with the American, and would have been

Khrushchev attempted to transform Soviet agriculture. In 1954 he proposed to increase deliveries to the state by 40 per cent. This could only be achieved by farming virgin land in harsh conditions in Siberia and Kazakhstan. A large number of *kolkhozes* (collective farms), such as the one shown in this aerial view, were set up in these regions, thanks to the arrival in the "new lands" of hundreds of thousands of young people.

even more visibly so but for a costly system of subsidies. Russian agriculture, which had once fed the cities of Central Europe and paid for the industrialization of the tsarist era, had been a continuing failure; paradoxically, the Soviet Union often had to buy American grain. The official Soviet Communist Party programme of 1961 proposed that by 1970 the USSR should have outstripped the United States in industrial output, but the proposal was not made reality (unlike President Kennedy's of the same year to put a man on the moon). Yet the USSR, in comparison with many undeveloped countries, was undoubtedly rich. In spite of the obvious disparity between them as consumer societies, to the poor the USA and USSR sometimes looked alike. Many Soviet citizens, too, were more aware of the contrast between their stricken and impoverished country in the 1940s with one much less so in the 1960s, than of comparison with the United States. Moreover, the contest of the two systems was not always one-sided. Soviet investment in education, for

Built in Moscow in the 12th century, the Kremlin was originally a fortress, but its use as state headquarters has made it synonymous with Soviet and now with Russian government.

example, was thought to have achieved literacy rates as good as, and even slightly higher at times, than the American. Such comparisons, which fall easily over the line from quantitative to qualitative judgement, nevertheless do not alter the basic fact that the per capita GDP of the Soviet Union still in the 1970s lagged far behind that of the United States. If its citizens had at last been given old-age pensions in 1956 (nearly half a century after the British people), they also had to put up with health services which fell further and further behind those available in the West. There had been a long legacy of backwardness and disruption to eliminate; only in 1952 had real wages in Russia even got back to their 1928 level. The theory of "convergence" was always too optimistic.

SOVIET SPACE EXPLORATION

By 1970 a scientific and industrial base existed in the Soviet Union which in scale and at its best matched that of the United States. Its most obvious expression, and a great

source of patriotic pride to the Soviet citizen, was the exploration of space. By 1980 there was so much ironmongery in orbit that it was difficult to recapture the startling impression made in 1957 by the first Soviet satellites. Although American successes had speedily followed, Soviet space achievements remained of the first rank. There seemed to be something in space exploration which fed the patriotic imagination and rewarded patience with other aspects of daily life in the USSR. It is not too much to say that for some Soviet citizens their space technology justified the revolution; Russia was shown by it to be able to do almost anything another nation could do, and much that only one other could do, and perhaps one or two things which, for a while, no other could do. She was modernized at last.

SOCIAL STRAINS IN THE USSR

Whether Russia's modernization meant that she was in some sense becoming a satisfied nation, with leaders more confident and less suspicious of the outside world and less prone to disturb the international scene, is a different matter. Soviet responses to Chinese resurgence were not encouraging; there was talk of a pre-emptive nuclear attack on the Chinese border. Soviet society was beginning to show new signs of strain, too, by 1970. Dissent and criticism, particularly of restraints upon intellectual freedom, had become obvious for the first time in the 1960s. So did symptoms of anti-social behaviour, such as hooliganism, corruption and alcoholism. But such defects probably held both as much and as little potential for significant change as in other large countries. Less spectacular facts may turn out to be more important in the long run; later perspectives may reveal that one important watershed was passed in the 1970s, when native Russian speakers for the first time became a minority in the Soviet Union. Meanwhile, the Soviet Union remained a police state where the limits of freedom and the basic privileges of the individual were defined in practice by an apparatus backed up by administrative decisions and political prisons. The real difference between the Soviet Union and the United

States (or any West European nation) was still best shown by such yardsticks as her enormous expenditure on jamming foreign broadcasting.

AMERICAN SOCIETY

FOR OBVIOUS REASONS, changes in the United States were more easily observed than those in the Soviet Union, but this did not always make it easier to discern fundamentals. Of the sheer growth of American

The Soviet dissident scientist Andrei Sakharov (1921–1989) is pictured in 1989, three years after Gorbachev authorized him to return from "exile" in Gorky, where he had been since 1980. Many intellectuals, artists and writers who openly criticized the régime were put under house arrest or exiled from the USSR.

Under Brezhnev, the USSR was a conservative society and the state used censorship, repression and the highly efficient secret police force (the KGB, whose headquarters in Moscow is seen here) to prevent all but a few outbreaks of unrest. When minor disturbances erupted, they were rapidly quashed by the use of force.

power there can be no doubt, nor of its importance to the world. In the middle of the 1950s the United States contained about six per cent of the world's population but produced more than half the world's manufactured goods. In 1968 the American population passed the two hundred million mark (in 1900 it had been seventy-six million), only one in twenty of whom were not native-born (though within ten years there would be worries about a huge Spanish-speaking immigration from Mexico and the Caribbean). Numbers of births went up while the birth-rate dropped after 1960; the United States was unique among major developed countries in this respect. Nearly a quarter of all births in 1987 were to unmarried women. More Americans than ever lived in cities or their suburbs, and the likelihood that they would die of some form of malignancy had trebled since 1900; this, paradoxically, was a sure sign of improvement in public health, because it showed a growing mastery of other diseases.

Built in the 1950s, Philadelphia's Penn Center – a complex of high-rise office buildings, hotels and shopping centres – symbolizes the rejuvenation of the city that took place during that decade. By the 1960s, the United States as a whole was enjoying the benefits of its post-war economic "miracle".

THE US ECONOMY

The United States' immensely successful industrial structure was dominated in 1970 by very large corporations, some of them commanding resources and wealth greater than those of some nations. Concern was often expressed for the interests of the public and the consumer, given the weight in the economy of these giants. But no doubts existed about the economy's ability to create wealth and power. Though it was to be shown that it could not do everything that might be asked of it, American industrial strength was the great constant of the post-war world. It sustained the huge military potential upon which the conduct of American foreign policy inevitably rested.

American economic success was a good generator of political mythologies. President Truman's second administration and those of President Eisenhower were marked by noisy debate and shadow-boxing about the danger of governmental interference with free enterprise. This was beside the point. Ever since 1945 the federal government has held and indeed increased its importance as the first customer of the American economy. Government spending has been the primary economic stimulant and the goal of hundreds of interest groups, and hopes of balanced budgets and cheap, business-like administration always ran aground upon this fact. What was more, the United States was a democracy; whatever the doctrinaire objections to it, and however much rhetoric might be devoted to attacking it, the welfare state slowly advanced because voters wanted it that way. These facts made the old ideal of free enterprise unchecked and uninvaded by the influence of government more unrealistic than ever in the 1950s and 1960s. They also helped to prolong the Democratic coalition. The Republican presidents who were elected

in 1952 and 1968 on each occasion benefited from war-weariness and neither was able to persuade Americans that they should also elect Republican congresses. On the other hand, signs of strain were to be seen in the Democratic bloc before 1960 – Eisenhower appealed to many southern voters – and by 1970 something a little more like a national conservative party had appeared under the Republican banner because some Southerners had been offended by Democratic legislation on behalf of the black population. Twenty years later, though, the Democratic-voting "Solid South" created by the Civil War had disappeared as a political constant.

THE ELECTION OF PRESIDENT KENNEDY

Presidents could sometimes shift emphasis. The Eisenhower years leave an impression that little happened in the domestic history of the United States during them; it was not part of that president's vision of his office that he should provide a strong policy lead at home. Partly because of this, Kennedy's election by a narrow margin of the popular vote

The United States, which had access to enormous funds for basic and applied research, spearheaded the technological revolution of the 1960s and 1970s. Here, engineers and researchers demonstrate a drilling system that has huge implications for oceanographic research and the oil industry.

in 1960 – the arrival of a new man (and a young one, too) – produced a sense of striking change. Too much was made at the time of the more superficial aspects of this, but in retrospect it can be agreed that both in foreign and domestic affairs, the eight years of renewed Democratic rule from 1961 brought great change to the United States, though not in the way in which Kennedy or his vice-president, Lyndon Johnson, hoped when they took office.

BLACK AMERICANS' PROBLEMS

ONE ISSUE ALREADY present in American politics in 1960 was what could still then be called the Negro question. A century after emancipation, the black American was likely to be poorer, more often on relief, more often unemployed, less well-housed and less healthy than the white American. Thirty years later, this was still, and, sadly, even more the

case. In the 1950s, though, there was widespread optimism about changing things. The position of black people in American society suddenly began to appear intolerable and became a great political question because of three facts. One was migration. This turned a local Southern question into a national problem. Between 1940 and 1960 the black population of Northern states almost trebled. New York became the state with the biggest black population of the Union. This brought black Americans into view not only in new places, but in new ways. It revealed that the problem facing them was not only one of legal rights, but more complex; it involved economic and cultural deprivation, too. The second fact pushing the question forward on to the national stage lay outside the United States. Many of the new nations which were becoming a majority at the UN were nations of coloured peoples. It was an embarrassment – of which Communist propaganda always made good use – for the United States to display at home so flagrant a contravention of the ideals she espoused abroad as was provided by the plight of many of her black citizens. Finally, the action of black Americans themselves under their own leaders, some inspired by Gandhian principles of passive resistance to oppression, won over many white Americans. In the end the legal and political position of black Americans was radically altered for the better as a result. Bitterness and resentment were not eliminated in the process, though, but in some places actually increased and more black people than before remained evidently poor and actually deprived.

THE CIVIL RIGHTS CAMPAIGN

The first and most successful phase of the campaign for equal status of black Americans

While pro-segregation white students shout abuse at her, Elizabeth Eckford makes her way between lines of US National Guardsmen in an attempt to gain entrance to the "white" high school in Little Rock, Arkansas, in 1967.

Martin Luther King

Martin Luther King (1929–1968) was born in Alabama, the son of a Baptist clergyman. While studying at the Theological School of Boston University, he founded the Student Non-Violent Coordinating Committee (SNCC) and, with the help of the Association for the Advancement of Coloured People (NAACP), he organized a series of boycotts against segregation in public toilets in Montgomery (Alabama) which brought him national recognition.

King led the non-violent civil rights movement with tremendous energy, culminating in 1963 in the great march on Washington, DC, where he gave his most famous speech in front of a crowd of almost 300,000 people of every race. "I have a dream," he declared, "that my four little children will one day live in a nation where they will not be judged by the colour of their skin but by the content of their character."

Nominated "Man of the Year" by *Time* magazine in 1963 and awarded the Nobel Peace Prize in 1964, King continued to organize acts of resistance in order to ensure that anti-segregationist laws were complied with. He did not agree with organizations that advocated violence as the only way to bring about change, nor did he accept Malcolm X's black nationalism. In 1968 King led a series of peaceful demonstrations in Memphis, and on 4 April he was assassinated in that city while he stood on a hotel balcony.

Martin Luther King delivers his "I have a dream" speech on the steps of the Lincoln Memorial in Washington, DC.

was a struggle for "civil rights", of which the most important were the unhindered exercise of the franchise (always formally available, but actually not, in some Southern states) and access to equality of treatment in other ways. The success stemmed from decisions of the Supreme Court in 1954 and 1955. The process thus began not with legislation but with judicial interpretation. These important first decisions provided that the segregation of different races within the public school system was unconstitutional and that where it existed it should be brought to an end within a reasonable time. This challenged the social system in many Southern states, but by 1963 some black and white children were attending public schools together in every state of the Union, even if others stayed in all-black or all-white schools.

Legislation was not really important until after 1961. After the inauguration of a successful campaign of "sit-ins" by black leaders (which itself achieved many important local victories) Kennedy initiated a programme going beyond the securing of voting rights to attack segregation and inequality of many kinds. It was to be continued by his successor. Poverty, poor housing, bad schools in run-down urban areas were symptoms of deep dislocations inside American society, and were inequalities made more irksome by the increasing affluence in which they were set.

Children survey the aftermath of the race riots that shook Los Angeles in 1992. Three days of unrest followed the news that four local white policemen had been acquitted of the beating of a black motorist, Rodney King, although they had been caught on film.

The Kennedy administration appealed to Americans to see their removal as one of the challenges of a "New Frontier".

SOCIAL AND ECONOMIC DIFFICULTIES

Even greater emphasis was given to legislation to remove poverty and its accompanying problems by Johnson, who succeeded to the presidency when Kennedy was murdered in November 1963. Unhappily, laws did not help; the deepest roots of the black American problem appeared to lie beyond their reach in what came to be called the "ghetto" areas of great American cities. The perspective from 1990 is again helpful. In 1965 (a hundred years after emancipation became law throughout the whole United States) a ferocious outbreak of rioting in a

district of Los Angeles with a large black population was estimated to have involved at its height as many as 75,000 people. Other troubles followed in other cities, but not on the same scale. Twenty-five years later, all that had happened in Watts (where the Los Angeles outbreak took place) was that conditions had further deteriorated. By 1990 Los Angeles police were regarded there as members of an occupying army: they were in that year authorized to add dum-dum bullets to their already formidable weaponry. Over the United States as a whole a young black male American of the 1990s was seven times as likely to be murdered as his white contemporary (and probably by another black man). He was more likely to experience a term in prison than to go to a university. By then, too, two-thirds of black babies were born to unmarried mothers. The problem was (it was usually agreed) one of economic opportunity, but none the easier to solve for that. It not only remained unsolved but appeared to be running away from solution. The poisons it secreted burst out in crime, a major collapse in health standards in some black communities, and in ungovernable and virtually unpoliceable inner-city areas. In the culture and politics of white America they seemed at times to have produced a near-neurotic obsession with colour and racial issues.

His own poor Southern background had made Johnson a convinced and convincing exponent of the "Great Society" in which he discerned America's future and perhaps this might have held promise for the handling of the black economic problem had he survived. Potentially one of America's great reforming presidents, Johnson nevertheless experienced tragic failure, for all his aspirations, experience and skill. His constructive and reforming work was soon forgotten (and, it must be said, set aside) when his presidency came to

be overshadowed by an Asian war disastrous enough before it ended to be called by some America's Sicilian Expedition.

THE VIETNAM WAR

AMERICAN POLICY in Southeast Asia under Eisenhower had come to rest on the dogma that a non-Communist South Vietnam was essential to security, and that it had to be kept in the Western camp if others in the area – perhaps as far away as India and Australia – were not to be subverted. So, the United States had become the backer of its conservative government. President Kennedy did not question this view. He began to back up American military aid with "advisers". By the time of his murder there were 23,000 of them in South Vietnam, and, in fact, many of them were in action in the field. President Johnson followed the course already set,

In 1966, the Americans attempted to "pacify" rural areas controlled by the Vietcong through search-and-destroy missions in the lowlands. While refugees fled to the cities, the Americans also used chemicals to destroy the foliage that sheltered the rebels in the jungles. Here, American troops from the 173rd Battalion disembark from helicopters to launch an operation.

believing that pledges to other countries had to be shown to be sound currency. But government after government in Saigon turned out to be broken reeds. At the beginning of 1965 Johnson was advised that South Vietnam might collapse; he had the authority to act (given him by Congress after North Vietnamese attacks on American ships the previous year) and air attacks were launched against targets in North Vietnam. Soon after, the first official American combat units were sent to the South. American participation quickly soared out of control. In 1968 there were over 500,000 American servicemen in Vietnam; by Christmas that year a heavier tonnage of bombs had been dropped on North Vietnam than fell on Germany and Japan together in the entire Second World War.

The outcome was politically disastrous. It was almost the least of Johnson's worries that the American balance of payments was wrecked by the war's huge cost, which also took money from badly needed reform projects at home. Worse was the bitter domestic outcry which arose as casualties mounted and attempts to negotiate seemed to get nowhere. Rancour grew, and with it the alarm of moderate America. It was small consolation that Russia's costs in supplying arms to North Vietnam were heavy, too.

DISILLUSION IN THE UNITED STATES

More was involved in domestic uproar over Vietnam than the agitation of young people rioting in protest and distrust of their government or the anger of conservatives who found their ideals outraged by ritual desecrations of the symbols of patriotism and refusals to carry out military service. Vietnam was bringing about a transformation in the way many Americans looked at the outside world. It was in Southeast Asia that it was at last borne in on the thoughtful that even the United States could not obtain every result she wanted, far less obtain it at any reasonable cost. The late 1960s were a sunset era, though the sunset was not of American power but rather of the illusion that American power was limitless and irresistible. Americans had approached the post-war world with this illusion intact. Their country's strength had, after all, decided two world wars. Beyond them there stretched back a century and a half of virtually unchecked and unhindered continental expansion, of immunity from European intervention, of the growth of an impressive hegemony in the American hemisphere. There was nothing in American history which was wholly disastrous or irredeemable, hardly anything in which there was, ultimately, failure, and nothing over which most Americans felt any guilt. It had been easy and natural for

A crowd of demonstrators gathers in front of the Pentagon brandishing posters with anti-Vietnam War slogans in 1967.

that background to breed a careless assumption of limitless possibility and for that to be carried over from domestic to foreign concerns. It was understandable that Americans should forget the special conditions of continental isolation and the supremacy of British sea-power on which their success story had long been built.

THE END OF THE VIETNAM WAR

The reckoning had begun to be drawn up in the 1950s, when many Americans had to be content with a lesser victory in Korea than they had hoped for. There had then opened twenty years of frustrating dealings with nations often enjoying not a tenth of the power of the United States but apparently able to thwart her. At last, in the Vietnam disaster, both the limits of power and its full costs were revealed. In March 1968 the strength of domestic opposition to the war was shown clearly in the primary elections. Johnson had already drawn the conclusion that the United States could not win, had restricted bombing and asked the North to open negotiations again. Dramatically, he also announced that he would not stand for re-election in 1968. Just as the casualties of the Korean War won Eisenhower election in 1952, so the casualties of Vietnam, on the battlefield and at home, helped to elect another Republican president in 1968 (only four years after a huge Democratic majority for Johnson) and to re-elect him in 1972. Vietnam was not the only factor, but it was one of the most important in dislocating the old Democratic coalition.

The new president, Mr Richard Nixon, began to withdraw American ground forces from Vietnam soon after his inauguration. Peacemaking took three years. In 1970 secret negotiations began between North Vietnam

and the United States, accompanied by further withdrawals but also by renewed and intensified bombing of the North by the Americans. The diplomacy was tortuous and difficult. The United States could not admit it was abandoning its ally, though in fact it had to do so, nor would the North Vietnamese accept terms which did not leave them with power to harass the Southern régime through their sympathizers in the South. Amid considerable public outcry in the United States, bombing was briefly resumed at the end of 1972, but for the last time. Soon afterwards, on 27 January, 1973, a cease-fire was signed in Paris.

The Vietnam War created hundreds of thousands of refugees, including these Eurasian and Afro-Asian orphans (pictured at an orphanage in An-Loi in 1972), left behind by the departing US army.

Civilians are rounded up by US Marines inside the Citadel in Hué during the Vietcong's costly but politically successful "Tet Offensive" in early 1968. This surprise attack on South Vietnamese cities, launched to coincide with the Vietnamese New Year (Tet), was the turning-point of the Vietnam War. After months of optimistic reports from Saigon, the American people were dismayed to hear that the "defeated" Vietcong were occupying no less than 103 towns and had penetrated even the US embassy in Saigon. Although they were quickly repulsed, the effect on US policy-makers was decisive. They had learned that the Communists would make any sacrifice to win. Victory cost North Vietnam and the Vietcong a total of nearly one million combatant deaths.

THE EFFECTS OF THE CEASE-FIRE

The Vietnam War had cost the United States vast sums of money and 58,000 dead. It had gravely damaged American prestige, had eroded American diplomatic influence, had ravaged domestic politics and had frustrated reform. What had been achieved was a brief preservation of a shaky South Vietnam saddled with internal problems which made its survival uncertain, while terrible destruction had been inflicted on the peoples of Indo-China. Perhaps the abandonment of the illusion of American omnipotence offsets these costs.

It was at least a domestic success to disentangle the United States from the morass and President Nixon reaped the benefit. The liquidation of the venture had followed other signs of his recognition of how much the world had already changed since the Cuban crisis. The most striking was a new policy of normal and direct relations with China. It came to a climax with a visit of the president to China in February 1972. It was not only an attempt to start to bridge what he described as "16,000 miles and twenty-two years of hostility" (he might have added "and 2,500 years of history"), but the first visit by an American president to mainland Asia. Diplomatic relations with the United States at the highest level were paralleled by another gain for China, her entry to the United Nations Organization and a seat on the Security Council.

When Mr Nixon followed his Chinese trip by becoming also the first American president to visit Moscow (in May 1972) and this was followed by an interim agreement on arms limitation, the first of its kind, it seemed that another important change had come about. The stark polarized simplicities of the Cold War were clearly gone, however doubtful might be what came next. The Vietnam settlement followed and can hardly have been

unrelated to it; Moscow and Peking both had to be squared if there were to be a cease-fire. China's attitude to the Vietnamese struggle was, we may guess, by no means simple; it was complicated by the potential danger from Soviet policy, by the United States' use of its power elsewhere in Asia, notably Taiwan and Japan, and by Vietnamese nationalism. For all China's help, its Indo-Chinese Communist satellite could not be trusted. The Vietnamese had a history of struggle against Chinese as well as French imperialism. In the immediate aftermath of the American withdrawal, too, the nature of the struggle going on in Vietnam (and now spread to Cambodia) was more and more clearly revealed as a civil war.

RENEWED CONFLICT IN VIETNAM

The North Vietnamese did not wait long before resuming operations. For a time the United States government had to pretend not to see this; there was too much relief at home

Former Saigon régime officers attend a "re-education" class in a South Vietnamese work camp in 1976. The North Vietnamese officer, through his loud-speaker, assures the prisoners that, if they learn by rote the declarations he is brandishing, they will be guaranteed reassimilation into the new Vietnam. For many of these officers, however, freedom was still years away.

over the liquidation of the Asian commitment for scruples to be expressed over the actual observation of the peace terms which had made withdrawal possible. When a political scandal forced Nixon's resignation, his successor faced a Congress suspicious of what it saw as dangerous foreign adventures and determined to thwart them. This meant that there would be no attempt to uphold the peace terms of 1972 in so far as they guaranteed the South Vietnamese régime against overthrow.

Early in 1975 American aid to Saigon came to an end. A government which had lost virtually all its other territory was reduced to a backs-to-the-wall attempt to hold the capital city and lower Mekong with a demoralized and defeated army. At the same time, Communist forces in Cambodia were destroying another régime earlier supported by the United States. Congress prevented the sending of further military and financial help. The pattern of China in 1947 was being

repeated; the United States was eventually to cut her losses at the expense of those who had relied on her (though 117,000 Vietnamese left with the Americans).

Such an outcome was doubly ironical. In the first place it seemed to show that the hardliners on Asian policy had been right all along – that only the knowledge that the United States was in the last resort prepared to fight for them could guarantee the post-colonial régimes' resistance to Communism. Secondly, the swing back to isolationism in the United States was accentuated, not muffled, by defeat and disaster; those who reflected on the American dead and missing and the huge cost now saw the whole Indo-China episode as a pointless and unjustifiable waste on behalf of peoples who would not fight to defend themselves. Yet an alternative reading of the American position in East Asia was possible. It was arguable that better relations with China mattered much more than the loss of Vietnam.

CONFLICTING SIGNS IN THE US

By the end of the 1970s, America and her allies were confused and worried. The situation was not easy to read. Objectively, though, there were good grounds for reassurance. The American democratic system showed no sign of breaking down, or of not meeting many of the country's needs, even if it could not find answers to all its problems. The economy had, astonishingly, been able to continue for years to pay for a hugely expensive war, for a space exploration programme that put men on the moon, and for the maintenance of garrisons around the world on an unprecedented scale. True, the black American's plight continued to worsen, and some of the country's greatest cities seemed stricken by urban decay, while a deep psychological wound had been inflicted by the Vietnam War on those who had hitherto believed unquestioningly in the traditions of

American patriotism. Fewer Americans, though, seemed to find such facts so worrying as their country's supposed military inferiority (essentially, in missiles) to the Soviet Union (it was to be an issue in the presidential election of 1980). Concern was exacerbated by the undermining in the early 1970s of confidence in the traditional leadership of the president in foreign affairs by domestic scandal and a new distrust of the executive power. President Ford (who had taken office in 1974 on the resignation of his predecessor) had already had to face a Congress unwilling to countenance further aid to its allies in Indo-China. When Cambodia collapsed, and South Vietnam quickly followed, questions began to be asked at home and abroad about how far what looked like a worldwide retreat of American power might go. If the United States would no longer fight over Indo-China, would she, then, do so over Thailand? More alarmingly still, would she fight over Israel –

Pol Pot, pictured here with one of his Khmer Rouge soldiers, headed a notoriously bloodthirsty pro-Chinese régime in Cambodia from 1976 until 1979. In 1978 the Vietnamese invasion of Cambodia accelerated the deterioration of relations between Vietnam and China and led to the frontier war of February–March 1979. When the victorious Vietnamese overthrew his régime, Pol Pot became the leader of the Communist resistance movement, which is active today.

Richard Nixon (1913–1994) had been US president for six years when this photograph was taken in 1974 at the height of the Watergate scandal that cost him his political career. He is shown in the last minutes of his presidency, before his resignation in favour of Gerald Ford.

or even Berlin? There were good reasons to think the Americans' mood of resignation and dismay would not last for ever, but while it lasted, their allies looked about them and felt uneasy.

TWO EUROPES

EUROPE WAS THE BIRTHPLACE of the Cold War and for a long time its main theatre. Yet well before 1970 there had been signs that the terrible simplifications institutionalized in NATO and (more rigidly still) in the Warsaw Pact might not be all that was shaping history there. Even in Eastern Europe, seemingly long insulated by Soviet power from external stimuli to change and by its command economies, there were signs of division. The violence with which Albania, the tiniest of Europe's Communist countries, condemned the Soviet Union and applauded China when the two fell out in the 1960s had to be endured by the Russians; Albania had no frontier with other Warsaw Pact countries and so was not likely to have to take account of the Red Army. It was more striking when Romania, with Chinese support, successfully contested the direction of her economy by COMECON, asserting a national right to develop it in her own interest. She even took up a vaguely neutralist position on questions of foreign policy – though remaining inside the Warsaw Pact – and did so, oddly enough, under a ruler who imposed on his people one of the most rigidly dictatorial régimes in Eastern Europe. But Romania (unlike Albania) had no land frontier with a NATO country, and one eight hundred kilometres with Russia; her skittishness could be tolerated, therefore. That there were clear limits to the dislocation of the old monolithic unity of Communism was none the less shown in 1968. When a Communist government in Czechoslovakia set about liberalizing its internal structure and developing trade relations with West Germany, tolerance was not forthcoming. After a series of attempts to bring her to heel Czechoslovakia was invaded in August 1968 by Warsaw Pact forces. To avoid a repetition of what had happened in Hungary in 1956, the Czech government did not resist and a brief attempt to provide an example of "socialism with a human face", as a Czech politician had put it, was obliterated.

POLYCENTRISM

Sino-Soviet tension combined with tremblings within the Eastern bloc and the uneasiness of the United States over relations with Latin American countries to lead to suggestions that the world as a whole was abandoning bipolarity for "polycentrism" as an Italian Communist put it. The loosening of Cold War simplicities had indeed been surprising. Another complicating development had meanwhile emerged in Western Europe, the region where the evolution of a unified world history had actually begun. In 1980 it was clear that one of the historic roles of the peoples of that part of the continent was over. Western Europeans by then ruled no more of the world's surface than their ancestors had done five hundred years earlier. Huge transformations had taken place, and irreversible things had been done in those five centuries. But Europe's imperial past was over. Yet the discovery of a new role for her was already well under way. Thirty years earlier, in the 1950s, Western Europe had begun to show some of the earliest signs, feeble though they were, that nationalism's grip on the human potential for large-scale organization might be loosening in the very place where nationalism had been born.

of France. The likelihood of another great civil war in the West over the German question had receded. Soviet policy had also given the Western countries many new reasons to cooperate more closely; what happened in Eastern Europe in the late 1940s struck them as a warning of what might happen if the Americans ever went home and they remained divided. The Marshall Plan and NATO therefore turned out to be only the first two of many important steps towards an integration whose heart was to be found in a new Europe.

In the "Prague Spring" of 1968 mass demonstrations, such as the one pictured here, were held in Prague, demanding the liberalization of the régime. The arrival of Soviet tanks in August to quell the unrest, however, quashed the attempt at democratization.

WESTERN EUROPEAN INTEGRATION

THE LEGACIES of common experience which have shaped Western Europe have been, not unreasonably, traced by enthusiasts back to the Carolingians, but 1945 is far enough to go back at this point. From that date, the decisive agents for more than forty years had been the outcome of war and Soviet policy. They had ended by partition the German problem. This quietened the old fears

NEW EUROPEAN INSTITUTIONS

Western European integration had more than one source. The initiation of the Marshall Plan was followed by the setting-up of an Organization (at first of sixteen countries, but later expanded) of European Economic Cooperation in 1948, but the following year, a month after the signing of the treaty setting up NATO, the first political bodies representing ten different European states were also set

Post-war Europe: economic and military blocs 1949–91

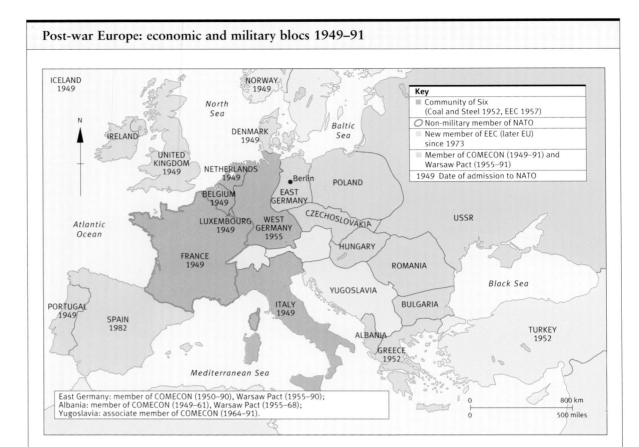

Key
- Community of Six (Coal and Steel 1952, EEC 1957)
- ○ Non-military member of NATO
- New member of EEC (later EU) since 1973
- Member of COMECON (1949–91) and Warsaw Pact (1955–91)
- 1949 Date of admission to NATO

East Germany: member of COMECON (1950–90), Warsaw Pact (1955–90);
Albania: member of COMECON (1949–61), Warsaw Pact (1955–68);
Yugoslavia: associate member of COMECON (1964–91).

Following the end of the Second World War, the division of Europe was evident on a political and military level, with NATO opposing the Warsaw Pact. It was also evident in the European countries' economic organization: Western Europe, with the Marshall Plan and later the EEC, formed a stark contrast to the Eastern bloc countries, which were members of COMECON (the Council for Mutual Economic Assistance created by Stalin). Cuba, Mongolia and Vietnam were also members of COMECON, which was disbanded in 1991 when Communism collapsed in Europe.

up under a new Council of Europe. The economic forces making for integration were developing more rapidly, though. Customs Unions had already been created in 1948 between the "Benelux'" countries (Belgium, the Netherlands, and Luxembourg), and (in a different form) between France and Italy. The most important of the early steps towards economic integration, though, emerged from a French proposal for a Coal and Steel Community. This came into existence formally in 1951 and embraced France, Italy, the Benelux countries and, most significantly, West Germany. It made possible the rejuvenation of the industrial heartland of Western Europe and was the major step towards the integration of West Germany into a new international structure. Through economic arrangement, there came into existence the means of containing while reviving West Germany, whose strength, it was becoming clear, was needed in a Western Europe menaced by Soviet land-power. Under the influence of events in Korea, American official opinion (to the consternation of some Europeans) was in the early 1950s rapidly coming round to the view that Germany had to be rearmed.

THE ESTABLISHMENT OF THE EEC

Other facts, too, helped to ease the way to supranational organization in Europe. The political weakness symptomized by their domestic Communist parties subsided in both France and Italy, mainly thanks to economic recovery. Communists had ceased to take part in their governments as early as 1947 and the danger that French and Italian democracy might suffer a fate like Czechoslovakia's had disappeared by 1950. Anti-Communist opinion tended to coalesce about parties whose integrating forces were either Roman Catholic politicians or social democrats well aware of the fate of their comrades in Eastern Europe. Broadly speaking, these changes meant that Western Europe governments of a moderate right-wing complexion pursued similar aims of economic recovery, welfare service provision, and Western European integration in practical matters during the 1950s.

Further institutions emerged. In 1952 a European Defence Community formalized West Germany's military position. This was to be replaced by German membership of NATO, but a major thrust towards greater unity, as before, was economic. The crucial step came in 1957: the European Economic Community (EEC or "Common Market") then came into being when France, Germany, Belgium, the Netherlands, Luxembourg and Italy joined in signing the Treaty of Rome. Some enthusiasts spoke of the reconstitution of Charlemagne's heritage. It spurred countries which had not joined the EEC to set up

The expansion of the European Union (1957–1995)

Key
- Founder nations in 1957
- Admitted in 1973
- Admitted in 1981
- Admitted in 1986
- Incorporated in 1990
- Admitted in 1995
- Applied for membership in 1995

The European Economic Community was renamed the European Union (EU) in 1994. By the end of the following year – 38 years after its foundation by the first six members – fifteen countries were EU members. This map shows membership of the European Union in 1995 and the date of each country's entry.

their own, looser and more limited, European Free Trade Association (EFTA) two and a half years later. By 1986, the six countries of the original EEC (by then it had become simply the EC – the word "Economic", significantly, had been dropped) were twelve; while EFTA had lost all but four of its members to it. Five years later still, and what was left of EFTA was envisaging merging with the EC.

Western Europe's slow but accelerating movement towards political unity demonstrated the confidence of those who made the arrangements that armed conflict could never again be an acceptable alternative to cooperation and negotiation between their countries. The era of Western European international war, rooted in the beginnings of the national state system, was over. Tragically, though recognizing that fact, Great Britain's rulers did not seize at the outset the chance to join in giving it institutional expression; their successors were twice to be refused admission to the EEC before finally joining it. Meanwhile, the Community's interests were steadily cemented together by a Common Agricultural Policy which was, to all intents and purposes, a huge bribe to the farmers and peasants who

were so important a part of the German and French electorates, and, later, to those of poorer countries as they became members.

FRANCE UNDER DE GAULLE

For a long time determined opposition to further integration, at the political as opposed to the economic level, came from France. It was expressed strongly by General de Gaulle, who returned to politics in 1958 to become president when the French republic was threatened with civil war over Algeria. His first task was to negotiate these rapids by carrying through important constitutional reforms. His next service to France was as great as any in his wartime career, the liquidation of her Algerian commitment in 1961. The legions came home, some disgruntled. The act freed both him and his country for a more vigorous international role, though a very negative one. De Gaulle's view of European consolidation was limited to cooperation between independent nation-states; he saw the EEC as above all a way of protecting French economic interests. He was quite prepared to strain the new organization badly to get his way. Further, he in effect twice vetoed British application to join it. Wartime experience had left de Gaulle with a deep distrust of the "Anglo-Saxons" and a belief, by no means ill-founded, that the British still hankered after integration with an Atlantic community embracing the United States, rather than with continental Europe. In 1964 he annoyed the Americans by exchanging diplomatic representatives with Communist China. He insisted that France go ahead with her own nuclear weapons programme, declining to be dependent on American patronage. Finally, after causing it much trouble, he withdrew from NATO. This, too, could be seen as the coming of "polycentrism" to the

General de Gaulle, pictured here greeting the German leader Konrad Adenauer in 1963, was, above all, a French patriot, determined to restore France to its former glory. His personal ambition for Europe was to free it from American patronage and to create an integrated organization based on respect for national sovereignty.

Western bloc. When de Gaulle resigned after an unfavourable referendum on further constitutional change in 1969, a major political force making for uncertainty and disarray in Western Europe disappeared. Those who led France for the next couple of decades, while trying to sound like him, proved less intransigent, although French policy still opposed the evolution towards a more complete cohesion both of a true Common Market, free from internal restraints on trade, and of a politically united Europe.

BRITISH UNCERTAINTIES

GREAT BRITAIN FINALLY JOINED the EEC in 1973, a recognition, at last, of the facts of twentieth-century history by the most conservative of the historic nation-states. The decision complemented the withdrawal from empire and acknowledged that the British strategic frontier lay no longer on the Rhine, but on the Elbe. It was the climax, though not the end, of an era of uncertainty which had lasted almost since 1945. For a quarter-century all British governments had tried and failed to combine economic growth, increased social service provision and a high level of employment. The second depended ultimately on the first, but when difficulty arose, the first had always been sacrificed to the other two. The United Kingdom was, after all, a democracy whose voters, greedy and gullible, had to be placated. The vulnerability of the traditional British economy's commitment to international trade was a handicap, too. Others were its old staple industries, starved of investment, and the deeply conservative attitudes of the people. Though the United Kingdom grew richer (in 1970 virtually no British manual worker had four weeks' paid holiday a year and ten years later a third of them did), it fell behind more and more other developed countries both in its wealth and in its rate of creating it. If the British had managed a decline in international power and the achievement of a rapid decolonization without the violence and domestic bitterness visible elsewhere, it remained unclear whether they could shake off the past in other ways and ensure themselves even a modest prosperity as a second-rank nation.

VIOLENCE AND UNREST IN IRELAND

One obvious and symptomatic threat to order and civilization was posed in Northern Ireland. So far as Parliament at Westminster was concerned, the great nineteenth-century issue of Home Rule had been laid to rest in 1921, when a peace treaty between Great Britain and the Irish Nationalist party, Sinn Fein, created a new Irish Free State, practically independent of Great Britain, though formally a dominion within the British Commonwealth. The new Irish republic was now the sovereign power for most of the island. This concession to Irish nationalism and its predominantly Roman Catholic supporters was balanced by concession to the

Street fighting takes place in Dublin during the civil war that followed the establishment of the Irish Free State in 1922.

predominantly Protestant population of Ulster, the northern six counties of the island, who remained part of the United Kingdom, represented in Parliament at Westminster, but with substantial practical autonomy which they used to entrench the Protestant position there.

This solution left devoted Nationalists deeply dissatisfied and, indeed, civil war at once followed in the new republic between those willing to accept the settlement and those who were against it; more Irishmen were killed by other Irishmen in that struggle than had died in the rebellion against the British. Seeking to achieve the unity of the whole island under the Dublin government, the Nationalists continued to agitate and to resort to murder and violence, even in mainland Great Britain. In 1931 the Dublin government declared the IRA (the Irish Republican Army, and the military wing of Sinn Fein) an illegal body. Unsurprisingly, terrorism provoked further hardening of

Protestant attitudes in Ulster, and a sectarian hegemony there expressed itself in huge electoral majorities and in discrimination (notably in employment) against the Catholic minority.

After 1945, the Catholic minority's protests about this situation grew ever more vocal. There were clear indications that natural population increase would be likely to bring about in due time the transformation of this minority into a majority. Yet detailed concessions made in London seemed unable to meet their grievances on the ground. Soon, Protestant and Catholic hooligans alike seemed bent on destroying their homeland rather than cooperate with their rivals. Lunatic nationalism was as alive in Ulster as ever and cost the lives of thousands of British citizens – soldiers, policemen and civilians, Protestant and Catholic, Irish, Scotch, and English alike – in the 1970s and 1980s. At last, after much disillusionment at false starts, there seemed in the mid-1990s to be a real

Masked IRA activists carry the coffin of the hunger striker Martin Hurson in 1972. By that time, the IRA were killing police officers and British soldiers on leave and planting bombs in Belfast. In August 1971, the British government had decreed internment without trial for captured terrorists, but this only served to increase opposition to British rule.

if slight chance at last of arriving at a settlement, for visibly, in spite of their language, Unionists and Nationalists alike were finding the struggle exhausting and the terrorists, Protestant and Republican alike, seemed to be beginning to recognize this.

Meanwhile, British party politics had in fact after 1922 ceased to be as disrupted by Irish questions as they had been before 1914. Outside Ulster, the British electorate became, as time passed, more and more preoccupied, rather, by material concerns. Inflation ran at unprecedented levels (the annualized rate 1970–80 was over 13 per cent) and gave new fierceness to industrial troubles in the 1970s, especially in the wake of the oil crisis. There was speculation about whether the country was "ungovernable" as a miners' strike brought down one government, while many leaders and interpreters of opinion seemed obsessed with the themes of social division. Even the question whether the United Kingdom should remain in the EEC, which was submitted to the revolutionary device of a referendum in June 1975, was often put in these terms. It was therefore all the more surprising to many politicians when the outcome was unambiguously favourable to continued membership. It was the first sign for a decade or so that the views of the country at large were not necessarily represented by those who were considered their spokesmen; it was also possible that it was a decision which would in the end prove a turning-point in the history of a once-great nation, by closing off one sequence of choices which would have flowed ineluctably from a reassertion of insularity.

THE INFLATIONARY THREAT

More bad times (economically speaking) lay immediately ahead; inflation (in 1975

Margaret Thatcher was British prime minister from 1979 to 1990. Her neo-liberal economic policy was widely seen as an attack on the advanced British welfare state and particularly on the National Health Service, but the "Iron Lady" won ardent supporters as well as fierce opponents by breaking the power of the unions to obstruct the pace of change.

running at 26.9 per cent in the wake of the oil crisis) was at last identified by government as the major threat. Wage demands by trades unions were anticipating inflation still to come and it began to dawn on some that the era of unquestioned growth in consumption was over. There was a gleam of light; a few years earlier vast oil fields had been discovered under the sea-bed off the coasts of northern Europe. In 1976 the United Kingdom became an oil-exporting nation. That did not at once help much; in the same year, a loan from the International Monetary Fund was required. When Mrs Thatcher, the country's (and Europe's) first woman prime minister and the first woman leader of a major political party (the Conservative), took office in 1979 she had, in a sense, little to lose; her opponents were discredited. So, many felt, were ideas which had been long accepted uncritically as the determinants of

Argentinian tank crews prepare to go into battle against their British counterparts on the Falkland Islands, which Argentina held for two months. The war cost 254 British and 712 Argentine lives.

British policy. A radical new departure for once really did seem to be a possibility. To the surprise of many and the amazement of some among both her supporters and her opponents, that is exactly what Mrs Thatcher was to provide in what was to prove the longest tenure of power of any British prime minister in the twentieth century.

THE FALKLANDS WAR

Not far into her premiership, Mrs Thatcher found herself in 1982 presiding unexpectedly over what may well have been Great Britain's last colonial war. The reconquest of the Falkland Islands after their brief occupation by Argentinian forces was a great feat of arms as well as a major psychological and diplomatic success. The prime minister's instincts to fight for the principles of international law and territorial sovereignty, and for the islanders' right to say by whom they should be governed, were well-attuned to the popular mood (whose more vociferous and vulgar manifestations displeased the more fastidious among her opponents). She also correctly judged the international possibilities. After an uncertain start (unsurprising, given its traditional sensitivity over Latin America) the United States provided important practical and clandestine help. Chile, by no means easy with her restive neighbour, was not disposed to object to British covert operations on the mainland of South America. More important, most of the EC countries supported the isolation of Argentina in the UN, and resolutions which condemned the Argentinian action. It was especially notable that the British had from the start the support (not traditionally offered so readily) of the French government, which knew a threat to international security and vested rights under international law when it saw one.

It now seems clear that Argentinian action had been encouraged by the misleading impressions of likely British reactions gained from British diplomacy in previous years (for this reason, the British foreign secretary resigned at the outset of the crisis). Happily, one political consequence was the fatal wounding in its prestige and cohesiveness of the military régime which had ruled Argentina since 1976. It was replaced at the end of 1983 by a constitutional and elected government. In the United Kingdom, Mrs Thatcher's prestige rose with national morale; abroad, too, her standing was enhanced, and this was important. For the rest of the decade it provided the country with an influence with other heads of state (notably the American president) which the raw facts of British strength could scarcely have sustained by themselves. Not everyone agreed that this influence was always advantageously deployed; in this sphere (and as perhaps in some others) a comparison with General de Gaulle is to the point. Like his, Mrs Thatcher's personal convictions, preconceptions and prejudices were always very visible and she, like him, was no European, if that meant allowing emotional or even practical commitment to Europe to blunt their respective visions of national interest.

THATCHERITE BRITAIN

In domestic affairs, the effects of Mrs Thatcher's policies will require a long perspective for their full evaluation. What can be discerned even now is that she transformed the terms of British politics, and perhaps of cultural and social debate, dissolving a long *bien-pensant* consensus about national goals. This, together with the undoubted radicalism of many of her specific policies, awoke both enthusiasm and an unusual animosity. For all

the rhetoric, though, she failed to achieve two of her most important aims, the reduction of public spending, and the withdrawal of central government from as much as possible of the national life. Though former pretensions to direct the economy were at last set aside, ten years after she took up office government was playing a greater, not a smaller, part in many areas of society, and the public money spent on health and social security had gone up in real terms by a third since 1979 (unfortunately for her, without satisfying greatly increased demands).

In 1990, many of her political colleagues had come to believe that although she had led the Conservative Party to three general election victories in a row (a unique achievement in British politics), she would be a vote-loser in the next contest, which could not be far away. Faced with the erosion of loyalty and support, she resigned. Her successor, Mr Major, was something of an unknown quantity, having not had a long exposure in the front ranks of politics. It seemed likely, though, that British policy might now become less obstructive in its approach to the Community and its affairs (and would certainly be less rhetorical in style).

Economic insecurity and fear caused by rising unemployment led to numerous strikes in Great Britain during the 1980s. These striking London nurses are demanding better working conditions and higher salaries.

THE GROWTH OF THE EC

THE 1970S HAD BEEN difficult years for all the members of the European Community (as the EEC had been renamed). Growth fell away and their individual economies reeled under the impact of the oil crisis. This contributed to institutional bickering and squabbling (particularly on economic and financial matters) which had reminded Europeans of the limits to any transcendence of bipolarity so far achieved. It continued in the 1980s and, coupled with uneasiness about the success of the Far Eastern economic sphere, dominated by Japan, and a growing realization that other nations would wish to join the ten, led to further crystallization of ideas about the Community's future. Many Europeans saw more clearly that greater unity, a habit of cooperation and increasing prosperity were prerequisites of Europe's political independence, but there was also an emerging sense that such independence would always remain hollow unless Europe, too, could turn herself into a superpower.

Comfort could be drawn from further progress in integration. In 1979, a month after Mrs Thatcher formed her government, the first direct elections to the European Parliament were already being held. Greece in 1981, Spain and Portugal in 1986, were soon to join the Community. In 1987 the foundations of a common European currency and monetary system were laid (though the United Kingdom did not agree) and it was settled that 1992 should be the year which would see the inauguration of a genuine single market, across whose national borders goods, people, capital and services were to move freely. Members even endorsed in principle the idea of European political union, though the British and French had notable

The Spanish prime minister Felipe González (centre) signs the Treaty of Madrid in 1985. This formalized his country's entry into the European Community – Spain's membership would become valid on the first day of the following year.

misgivings. This by no means made at once for greater psychological cohesion and comfort as the implications emerged, but it was an indisputable sign of progress of some sort.

THE MAASTRICHT TREATY

In December 1991 at Maastricht another step forward was taken when the EC members agreed on measures to integrate the Community further, though, again with reservations and special arrangements for the cautious British. By then a common monetary system restricting the independence of members in managing the devaluation or revaluation of their own currencies was already in place. This was a significant stride towards a Common European currency. As at every point in the Community's history, satisfaction about what has been achieved was almost lost to sight amid quarrels, misgivings, misinterpretations, ambiguities about what should or might lie ahead. Yet many other European nations were now knocking at or approaching the door of entry, a good testimony to what they saw as the advantages of membership. Since 1957, Western Europe had come a very long way, more, perhaps, than was always grasped by men and women born and grown to maturity since the Treaty of Rome had been signed. Underlying the institutional changes, too, were growing similarities – in politics, social structure, consumption habits and beliefs about values and goals. The old disparities of economic structure had greatly diminished, as the decline in numbers and increase in prosperity of French and German farmers showed. On the other hand, new problems had presented themselves as poorer and perhaps politically less stable countries had joined the EC. That there had been huge convergences could not be contested. What was still unclear was what

In 1997 German construction workers demonstrate against unemployment and against what they see as Chancellor Kohl's betrayal of their interests at the Maastricht conference.

this might imply for the future. With the uncertainties of the Maastricht debate behind them, the Community's members might have believed that due and uninterrupted progress would now be made towards the realization of its terms, but this was not to be the case. In 1992 the European Monetary System ran into heavy weather and after a brief but bruising experience of what the international currency speculators might do to the pound sterling, Mr Major's government withdrew from the Exchange Rate Mechanism which governed its currencies.

The experience exacerbated distrust in the United Kingdom of "the European project", as some called it, and there followed for the remainder of the life of the government increasing division in its own ranks and that of the party behind it which – together with the feeling in the end that eighteen years in office was long enough – brought it to devastating defeat at the polls in May 1997. There then took office a Labour government with a huge majority. Whatever might have been hoped of the conciliatory tone of its leaders towards the EU (by comparison with that of the Conservative Party spokesmen) the new government as a matter of practice continued to display much caution about suggestions of further integration and, in particular, about the proposal to introduce a common European currency in 1999 to which a majority of member governments of the EU were committed, albeit not always with much evidence of strong support from their electorates.

The West German chancellor Helmut Kohl (b.1930) and the French president François Mitterrand (1916–1996) are pictured at a European summit in Hanover in 1988. Kohl and Mitterrand had a close professional relationship, and often worked together to promote greater European integration.

4 NEW CHALLENGES TO THE COLD WAR WORLD ORDER

IN DECEMBER 1975 Mr Ford became the second American president to visit China. The adjustment of his country's deep-seated attitudes towards the People's Republic had begun with the slow recognition of the lessons of the Vietnam disaster. On the Chinese side, changes were to be understood also in a deeper perspective. They were a part of China's resumption of the international and regional role appropriate to her historical stature and potential. This can be said to have been going on since 1911, but could only come to fruition after 1949. In the 1970s it was completed. An approach could then be made towards establishing normal relations with the United States. It helped that the Chinese were concerned over Soviet policy, which was seen as expansionist and threatening. Formal recognition of what had been achieved came in 1978. In a Sino-American agreement the United States made the crucial concession that its forces should be withdrawn from Taiwan and that official diplomatic relations with the island's KMT government should be ended.

CHINA AFTER MAO

MAO HAD DIED in 1976. The threat of the ascendancy of a "gang of four" of his coadjutors (one was his widow) who had promoted the policies of the Cultural Revolution was quickly averted by their arrest (and, eventually, trial and punishment in 1981). Under new leadership dominated by Party veterans, it soon became clear that the excesses of the Cultural Revolution were to be corrected. In 1977 there rejoined the government as a vice-premier the twice previously disgraced Deng Xiaoping, firmly associated with the contrary trend. Scope was now to be given to individual enterprise and the profit motive, and economic connexions with non-Communist countries would be encouraged. The aim was to resume the process of technological and industrial modernization. The major definition of the new course was undertaken in 1981 at the plenary session of the central committee of the Party which met that year. It undertook, too, the delicate task of distinguishing the positive achievements of Mao, a "great proletarian revolutionary", from what it called his "gross

After Mao Tse-tung's death China entered a new phase. Before Deng Xiaoping took over the leadership of the Communist Party and the country, he had to overcome competition from the extreme left wing. The Gang of Four, his principal rivals, were arrested and imprisoned; Mao's widow, Jiang Qing, is pictured here at her trial, at which she was sentenced to death.

mistakes" and his responsibility for the set-backs of the Great Leap Forward and, more importantly, the Cultural Revolution.

MODERNIZATION

For all the comings-and-goings in CCP leadership, and the mysterious debates and sloganizing which continued to obscure polit-ical realities, and though Deng Xiaoping and his associates had to work through a collec-tive leadership which included conservatives, the 1980s were dominated by the new cur-rent. They settled the question which for thirty years had been at the heart of the Party's history, and therefore at the heart of China's, too. Modernization had at last been given precedence over Marxist socialism, even if that could hardly be said aloud (the secretary-general of the party pronounced in 1986 the amazing judgment that "Marx and Lenin cannot solve our problems", but he was dismissed soon afterwards), and even if much Marxist language still pervaded the rhetoric of government. Some said China was resuming the "capitalist road". This, too, was obscuring, though natural. There persisted in the Party and government a clear grasp of the need for positive planning of the economy; what was new was a recognition of its prac-tical limits and a willingness to try to discriminate more carefully between what was and was not within the scope of effective regulation in the pursuit of the major goals of economic and national strength, the improve-ment of living standards, and a broad egalitarianism.

One remarkable change was that agricul-ture was virtually privatized in the next few years in the sense that, although they did not own the freeholds of their land, peasants were encouraged to sell their produce freely in the markets. New slogans – "to get rich is

Deng Xiaoping (1904–1997) became a member of the Chinese Communist Party in 1925 and took part in the Long March. Deputy prime minister from 1952 and secretary of the Party's Central Committee, he resigned from political life in 1966 because of the personal criticism levelled against him during the Cultural Revolution. In 1973, he was appointed deputy president of the Party, and on Mao's death Deng effectively took over the leadership.

glorious" – were coined to encourage the development of village industrial and com-mercial enterprise, and a pragmatic road to development was signposted with "four modernizations". Special economic areas, enclaves for free trade with the capitalist world, were set up; the first was at Canton, the historic centre of Chinese trade with the West. It was not a policy without costs – grain production fell at first, inflation began to show itself in the early 1980s and foreign debt rose. Some blamed the growing visibility of crime and corruption on the new line.

ECONOMIC DEVELOPMENT

There can be no doubt of the development policy's economic success. Mainland China began in the 1980s to show that perhaps an economic "miracle" like that of Taiwan was within her grasp. By 1986 she was the second largest producer of coal in the world, and the

Pupils attend a Chinese secondary school in the Guizhou province. In 1949, China had illiteracy rates of up to 80 per cent, but the government's huge efforts to improve this situation have now borne fruit: 93 per cent of the present population has access to primary education and 51 per cent to secondary education. By 1987, the combination of education reforms and adult literacy campaigns had reduced China's illiteracy rate to 30.5 per cent.

fourth largest of steel. GDP rose at more than ten per cent a year between 1978 and 1986, while industrial output had doubled in value in that time. Per capita peasant income nearly tripled, and by 1988 the average peasant family was estimated to have about six months' income in the savings bank. Taking a longer perspective, the contrasts are even more striking, for all the damage done by the Great Leap Forward and the Cultural Revolution. The value of foreign trade multiplied roughly twenty-five times in per capita terms between 1950 and the middle of the 1980s. The social benefits which have accompanied such changes are also clear: increased food consumption and life expectancy, a virtual end to many of the great killing and crippling diseases of the old régime, and a huge inroad into mass illiteracy. China's continuing population growth was alarming and prompted stern measures of intervention, but it had not, as had India's, devoured the fruits of economic development.

INTERNATIONAL RELATIONS

The new Chinese line specifically linked modernization to strength. Thus it reflected the aspirations of China's reformers ever since the May 4th Movement, and of some even earlier. But China's international weight had already been apparent in the 1950s; what now happened was that it began to show itself in different ways. One important sign was agreement with the British in 1984 over terms for the reincorporation of Hong Kong on the expiration of the lease covering some of its territories in 1997. A later agreement with the Portuguese provided for the resumption of Macao, too. It was a blemish on the general recognition of China's due standing that Vietnam (with which China's relations at one time degenerated into open warfare, when the two countries were rivals for the control of Cambodia, traditionally part of the old imperial zone of Chinese hegemony) remained hostile to her among neighbouring countries; but the Taiwanese were somewhat reassured by Chinese promises that the reincorporation of the island in the territory of the republic in due course would not endanger its economic system. Similar assurances were given over Hong Kong. Like the establishment of special trading enclaves on the mainland where external commerce could flourish, such statements underlined the importance China's new rulers attached to commerce as a channel of modernization. China's sheer size gave such a policy direction importance over a wide area. By 1985 the whole of East and Southeast Asia constituted a single trading zone of unprecedented potential.

THE JAPANESE ECONOMY

WITHIN THE ASIAN TRADING ZONE, new centres of industrial and commercial activity were developing so fast in the 1980s as to justify by themselves the view that the old global balance of economic power had disappeared. South Korea, Taiwan, Hong

The Asian Tigers

Four so-called "Asian Tigers" – Taiwan, South Korea, Hong Kong and Singapore – enjoyed high growth rates during the 1970s, which contrasted with the crisis that affected industry in developed countries. Today, these four territories are among the most highly industrialized in the world. After 1970, all enjoyed a steady annual growth rate of around 7 per cent, in spite of the fact that they were oil importers and possessed only very limited natural resources.

The most revealing change in their economies occurred in exports. From representing only 1.4 per cent of world trade in 1964, these reached 5.7 per cent in 1983 and 8.4 per cent in 1989. By that year, all four centres were among the world's top 15 exporters of manufactured goods, particularly in areas such as footwear, textiles and clothes, electronic components, plastics and toys. The remarkable economic growth of the Asian Tigers is explicable in part by cultural factors, but also by the availability of large, cheap workforces, which made it possible for their industries to expand rapidly in the 1970s.

Workers assemble televisions in the Tatung television factory in Taipei, Taiwan.

Kong and Singapore had all shed any aura of undeveloped economies; Malaysia, Thailand and Indonesia were, by 1990, clearly moving up rapidly towards joining them. Their success was part of that of East Asia as a whole, and Japan had been indispensable to this outcome. The rapidity with which she, like China, recovered her former status as a power (and surpassed it) had obvious implications for her place both in the Asian and in the world balance. By 1970 the Japanese had the second-highest GDP in the non-Communist world. They had renewed their industrial base and had moved with great success into new areas of manufacture. Only in 1951 did a Japanese yard launch the country's first ship built for export; twenty years later, Japan had the largest shipbuilding industry in the world. At the same time she took a commanding position in consumer industries such as electronics and motor cars, of which Japan made more than any country

except the United States. This caused resentment among American manufacturers, the supreme compliment. In 1979 it was agreed that Japanese cars should be made in England, the beginning of penetration of the EEC market. The debit side of this account was provided by a fast-growing population and by the ample evidence of the cost of economic growth in the destruction of the Japanese environment and the wear and tear of urban life.

THE CHANGES IN JAPANESE SOCIETY

Japan was long favoured by circumstances. Vietnam, like Korea, was a stroke of luck. The American enforcement of a bias towards investment rather than consumption during the occupation years also helped. Yet human beings must act to take advantage of favourable circumstances, and Japanese attitudes were crucial. Post-war Japan could deploy intense pride and an unrivalled willingness for collective effort among her people; both sprang from the deep cohesiveness and capacity for subordinating the individual to collective purposes which had always marked Japanese society. Strangely, such attitudes seemed to survive the coming of democracy. It may be too early to judge how deeply democratic institutions are rooted in Japanese society; after 1951 there soon appeared something like a consensus for one-party rule (though irritation with this quickly expressed itself in the emergence of more extreme groupings, some anti-liberal). Mounting uneasiness was shown, too, over what was happening to traditional values and institutions. The costs of economic growth loomed up not only in huge conurbations and pollution, but in social problems which strained even Japanese custom. Great firms still operated with success on the basis of group loyalties buttressed by traditional attitudes and institutions. None the less, at a different level, even the Japanese family seemed to be under strain.

JAPAN'S NEW INTERNATIONAL STATUS

Economic progress also helped to change the context of Japanese foreign policy, which moved away in the 1960s from the simplicities of the preceding decade. Economic strength made the yen internationally important and drew Japan into the monetary diplomacy of Europe. Prosperity involved her in the affairs of many parts of the world. In the Pacific basin, she was a major consumer of other countries' primary produce; in the Middle East she became a large buyer of oil. In Europe, Japan's investment was thought alarming by some (even though her aggregate share was not large), while imports of her manufactured goods threatened European producers. Even food supply raised international questions; in the 1960s 90 per cent of Japan's requirements for protein came from fishing and this led to alarm that the Japanese might be over-fishing important grounds.

As these and other matters changed the atmosphere and content of foreign relations, so did the behaviour of other powers, especially in the Pacific area. Japan increasingly assumed in the 1960s a position in relation to other Pacific countries not unlike that of Germany towards Central and Eastern Europe before 1914. She became the world's largest importer of resources, too. New Zealand and Australia found their economies increasingly and profitably tied in to Japanese consumption rather than to the old British market. Both of them supplied meat, and Australia minerals, notably coal and iron ore.

The effects of overcrowding and the soaring price of real estate are illustrated in this view of houses built under a railway bridge in Tokyo.

On the Asian mainland the Russians and the South Koreans complained about the Japanese fishing. This added a new complication to an old story of economic involvement there. Korea was Japan's second biggest market (the United States was the biggest) and the Japanese started to invest there again after 1951. This at first revived a traditional distrust; it was ominous to find that South Korean nationalism had so anti-Japanese a tone that in 1959 the president of South Korea could urge his countrymen to unite "as one man" against not their northern neighbour, but Japan. Within twenty years, too, Japanese car manufacturers were looking askance at the vigorous rival they had helped create. As in Taiwan, so in Korea industrial growth had been built on technology diffused by Japan. Furthermore, Japan's dependence on imported energy had meant that she underwent a nasty economic shock when oil prices shot up in the 1970s. Yet these causes for concern did not seem to affect her progress. Japanese exports to the United States in 1971 were worth $6 billion; by 1984, that total had grown tenfold. By the end of the 1980s Japan was the world's second largest economic power in terms of GDP. As her industrialists turned to advanced information technology and biotechnology, and talked of running down car manufacturing, there was no sign that she had lost her power of disciplined self-adaptation.

FOREIGN POLICY

Greater strength had already meant greater responsibilities. The withdrawal of American direction was logically rounded off twenty years later when Okinawa (one of the first of her overseas possessions to be re-acquired) was returned to Japan. There remained the question of the Kuriles, still in Russian hands,

and of Taiwan, in the possession of the Chinese Nationalists and claimed by the Chinese Communists, but Japanese attitudes on all these matters remained – no doubt prudently – reserved. There was also the possibility that the question of Sakhalin might be reopened. All such issues began to look much more susceptible to revisions or at least reconsideration in the wake of the great changes brought to the Asian scene by Chinese and Japanese revival. The Sino-Soviet quarrel gave Japan much greater freedom for manoeuvre, both towards the United States, her erstwhile patron, and towards China and Russia. The embarrassment which too close a tie with the Americans might bring became clearer as the Vietnam War unrolled and political opposition to it grew in Japan. Her freedom was limited, in the sense that all three of the other great powers of the area were by 1970 equipped with nuclear weapons (and she, of all nations, had most reason to know their effect), but there was little doubt that Japan could produce them within a relatively brief time if she had to. Altogether, the Japanese stance had the potential to develop in various directions; in 1978 the Chinese vice-president visited Tokyo. In that year

Industry in Japan employs one third of the active population and is based on a structure in which huge ultramodern complexes co-exist with small family businesses. The motor industry, of which this Nissan factory forms a part, is one of the world's largest for utility vehicles and second only to the United States for saloon cars.

trade between China and Japan was worth as much as China's trade with the United States and West Germany combined. Indisputably, Japan was once more a world power.

INDIA

IF THE TEST OF A NATION'S STATUS as a world power is the habitual exercise of decisive influence, whether economic, military or political, outside its own geographical area, then by the 1980s India was clearly not one. This is perhaps one of the surprises of the second half of the century. India moved into independence with many advantages enjoyed neither by other former European dependencies, nor by Japan in the aftermath of defeat. She had in 1947 an effective administration, well-trained and dependable armed forces, a well-educated élite, thriving universities (some seventy of them), international benevolence and goodwill to draw upon and, soon,

the advantages of Cold War polarization to exploit. She had also then had poverty, malnutrition and major public health problems to confront, but so did China, and the contrast between the two countries by the 1980s was very great and even visible; the streets of Chinese cities were by 1970 filled by serviceably (though drably) dressed and well-nourished people, while those of India still displayed horrifying examples of poverty and disease.

INTERNAL DIVISIONS

In considering India's poor development performance it is easy to be pessimistically selective. There were sectors where growth was substantial and impressive. But such achievements are overshadowed by the fact that economic growth was followed closely by population increase; most Indians remained as poor as, or only a little better off than,

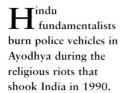

Hindu fundamentalists burn police vehicles in Ayodhya during the religious riots that shook India in 1990.

those who welcomed independence in 1947.

It has been argued that to have kept India together at all was a great achievement, given the country's fissiparous nature and potential divisions. But in the 1980s there were signs that even this success might prove not much longer durable. Sikh particularism brought itself vividly to the world's notice by the assassination of a prime minister in 1984, after the Indian army had carried out an attack on the foremost shrine of Sikh faith at Amritsar. In the next seven years, more than ten thousand Sikh militants, innocent bystanders, and members of the security forces were to be killed. Fighting with Pakistan over Kashmir, too, broke out again in the later part of the decade. In 1990 it was officially admitted that 890 people had died that year in Hindu–Muslim riots, the worst since 1947. It was an ominous symptom of reaction to the dangers of division that an orthodox and deeply conservative Hindu party made its appearance in Indian politics as the first plausible threat to the hegemony of Congress.

DYNASTIC POLITICS

The hegemony of Congress persisted, in spite of external threats. Congress forty years after independence was more visibly than ever not so much a political party in the European sense as an India-wide coalition of interest groups, notables and controllers of patronage, and this gave it, even under the leadership of Nehru, for all his socialist aspirations and rhetoric, an intrinsically conservative character. It was never the function of Congress, once the British were removed, to bring about change, but, rather, to accommodate it. This was in a manner symbolized by the dynastic nature of Indian government. Nehru had been succeeded as

India has been torn in recent decades by political infighting between the Congress Party and the Janata Party, border conflicts with Pakistan and religious struggles. Prime Minister Indira Gandhi was assassinated in 1984. She is pictured here with her son Rajiv, who was himself assassinated during the election campaign of 1991.

prime minister by his daughter, Mrs Indira Gandhi, and she, after her murder, by her son Rajiv Gandhi. When he, in turn, was blown up by an assassin (he was not in office at the time), Congress leaders almost at once showed an almost automatic reflex in seeking to persuade his widow to take up the leadership of the party.

Democracy nevertheless succeeded briefly in giving India governments other than those of Congress. Mrs Gandhi had been defeated in 1977 by the Janata Party, which then provided India with its first non-Congress government since independence. Her return to power in 1980 gave government back to Congress. Her son won an overwhelming electoral victory in 1985 and Congress continued in power until 1989 when elections produced a minority coalition (it, too, contained two members of the Nehru family) dependent on Janata and left-wing parties for its votes. On the other side of the coin, India's

For several months in 1984 armed Sikh extremists occupied the Golden Temple at Amritsar. The Indian army eventually laid siege to the building for three days, killing the extremists' leader, and leaving the 220-year old Sikh temple in ruins.

democratic record looked less firm after the authoritarianism showed by Mrs Gandhi in the 1970s (though it must be remembered that this led to her exclusion from office, even if not for long), or the recurrent use of president's powers to suspend normal constitutional government in specific areas, or the frequent brutalities of the police and security forces towards minorities. Under the Raj, Congress had sought for westernized Indians

the constitutional rights of Englishmen: it was not very successful in guaranteeing them after independence, far less in extending them to the non-westernized.

THE LEGACIES OF INDIA'S PAST

Once again, it is difficult not to return to the banal reflexion that the weight of the past was very heavy in India, and that no dynamic force emerged to throw it off. As memories of pre-independence India faded, the reassertion of India's tradition was always likely. Symbolically, when the moment for independence had come in 1947 it had been at midnight, because the British had not consulted the astrologers to provide an auspicious day and a moment between two days had therefore to be chosen for the birth of a new nation: it was an assertion of the power of Indian ways which were to lose little of their force in the next forty years. Partition had then redefined the community to be governed in much more dominantly Hindu terms. By 1980 the last Indian civil service officer recruited under the British had retired. India has still not reached the point at which it can feel assured of its modernization. It lives still with a conscious disparity between its ingrafted Western political system and the traditional society on which that has been imposed. For all the great achievements of many of its leaders, devoted men and women, the entrenched past, with all that means in terms of privilege, injustice and inequity, still stands in India's way. Perhaps those who believed in her future in 1947 were simply failing to recognize how difficult and painful fundamental change must be – and it is not for those of us who have found it so hard to accomplish much less fundamental change in our own society to be supercilious about that.

THE ISLAMIC WORLD

INDIA'S NEIGHBOUR PAKISTAN turned more consciously to some aspects of her own tradition – the Islamic – and in so doing participated in a movement of renewal which was visible across most of the Muslim world. Not for the first time, Western politicians have again had occasion in recent decades to recall that Islam is the creed of lands which stretch from Morocco in the west to China in the east. Indonesia, the largest Southeast Asian country, Pakistan, Malaysia and Bangladesh between them contain nearly half the world's Muslims. Beyond those countries and the Arabic lands, both the Soviet Union and Nigeria, the most populous African country, also had large numbers of Muslim subjects (as long ago as 1906, the tsarist government of Russia had been alarmed by revolution in Iran because of its possibly disturbing effect on the tsar's Muslim peoples). But new perceptions of the Islamic world took time to appear, and well into the 1970s the rest of the world thought mainly of the Arab countries of the Middle East, and especially of the oil-rich states among them, when it thought of Islam much at all.

THE COLD WAR AND ISLAM

So far as it went – and sensitivity to the area's problems was much heightened after the oil crisis of 1974 – the world's limited perception of the Islamic states was also for a long time obscured and confused by the perspectives of the Cold War. The shape of that conflict sometimes blurred into older frameworks, too; to some observers a traditional Russian desire for influence in the area seemed to be a strand in Soviet policy now nearer satisfaction than at any time in the past. The Soviet Union had by 1970 a worldwide naval

presence rivalling that of the United States and established even in the Indian Ocean, the only great maritime region in which Cold War confrontations had yet to occur. Following British withdrawal from Aden in 1967, that base had been used by the Russians with the concurrence of the South Yemen government. All this was taking place at a time when further south, too, there had been strategic setbacks for the Americans. The coming of the Cold War to the Horn of Africa and the former Portuguese colonies had added significance to events taking place further north.

THE MIDDLE EAST

Soviet policy, in a longer perspective, does not appear to have benefited much within the Muslim world from the disarray of the

In spite of its long-term exposure to Western influences, Indian society has never lost its deeply rooted traditions. Cows, considered sacred in the Hindu religion, are still a common presence in the streets of Bombay.

The faithful reach out to touch the Iranian religious and revolutionary leader Ayatollah Khomeini (1900–1989), on his return to Tehran in February 1979 after 15 years in exile. Khomeini quickly set up an Islamic republic and imprisoned or executed those who opposed the new régime.

Americans, marked though that was in the mid-1970s in the Middle East. Egypt had by then fallen out with Syria. She had turned to the United States in the hope of making a face-saving peace with Israel. When in 1975 the General Assembly of the United Nations denounced Zionism as a form of racism and granted the PLO "observer" status in the Assembly it was a consequence that Egypt was more and more isolated from other Arab states. By this time, the PLO's activity across the northern border was not only harassing Israel, but was steadily driving Lebanon, once a bastion of Western values, into ruin and disintegration. In 1978 Israel invaded southern Lebanon in the hope of ending the PLO raids. Though the non-Islamic world applauded when the Israeli and Egyptian prime ministers the following year met in Washington to agree a peace providing for Israel's withdrawal from Sinai, the Egyptian paid the price of assassination three years later by those who felt he had betrayed the Palestinian cause.

The limited settlement between Israel and Egypt owed much to President Carter, the Democratic candidate who had won the American presidential election of 1976. American morale was by then suffering from setbacks other than those in the Middle East. The Vietnam War had destroyed one president and his successor's presidency had been built on the management of American withdrawal and the 1973 settlement (though it was soon clear how little that settlement was worth). There was in the background, too, the fear many Americans shared of the rising strength of the USSR in ballistic missiles. All this affected American reactions to an almost wholly unforeseen event in 1979, which not only dealt a damaging blow to the United States, but revealed a potentially huge new dimension to the troubles of the Middle East. This was the overthrow of the shah of Iran.

THE IRANIAN REVOLUTION

Long the recipient of American favour as a reliable ally, in January 1979 the shah of Iran was driven from his throne and country by a coalition of outraged liberals and Islamic conservatives. An attempt to secure constitutional government soon collapsed as popular support rallied to the Islamic faction. Iran's traditional ways and social structure had been dislocated by a policy of modernization in which the shah had followed – with less caution – his father Reza Khan. Almost at once, there emerged a Shi'ite Islamic republic, led by an elderly and fanatical cleric. The United States quickly recognized the new régime, but unavailingly. It was tarred with guilt by association, as the patron of the former shah and the outstanding embodiment of capitalism and Western materialism. It was small consolation that the Soviet Union was soon undergoing similar vilification by the Iranian religious leaders, as the second "Satan" threatening the purity of Islam. Some Americans were encouraged, though, when the particularly ferocious Ba'ath régime in Iraq, already viewed with favour for its ruthless execution and pursuit of Iraqi Communists, fell out with the new Iran in a conflict inflamed (in spite of Ba'athist secularism) by the traditional animosity of Mesopotamian Sunni and Persian Shi'ite Muslims. It was in July 1979 that Saddam Hussein took over as president in Baghdad, and that looked encouraging to the State Department: he was likely to offset the Iranian danger in the Gulf, it seemed.

ANTI-WESTERN FEELING

The Iranian revolution implied more than just the American loss of a client state. Though a coalition of grievances had made possible the overthrow of the shah, a speedy reversion to archaic tradition (strikingly, in the treatment of women) showed that more than a ruler had been repudiated. The Iranian Islamic republic was also an expression of the rage, shared by many Muslims worldwide (especially in Arab lands), at the onset of secular western-ization and the failure of the promise of modernization. In the Middle East, as nowhere else, nationalism, socialism and capitalism had failed to solve the region's problems – or at least to satisfy passions and appetites they had aroused. Muslim funda-mentalists thought that Atatürk, Reza Khan and Nasser had all led their peoples down the wrong road. Islamic societies had successfully resisted the contagion of atheistic commu-nism but to many Muslims the contagion of the West now seemed even more threatening.

Paradoxically, the Western revolutionary notion of capitalist exploitation helped to feed this revulsion of feeling.

ISLAMIC FUNDAMENTALISM

The roots of Islamic fundamentalism (to use a crude blanket term) were varied and very deep. They could tap centuries of struggle against Christianity. They were refreshed from the 1960s onwards by the obviously growing difficulties of Western powers (including the USSR) in imposing their will on the Middle East and Persian Gulf, given their Cold War divisions. There was the mounting evidence for many Arabs that the Western principle of nationality advocated since the 1880s as an organizational remedy for the instability which followed Turkish decline had not worked (only too evidently in the 1980s, it would be clear that the wars of the Ottoman succession were not over). A favourable conjunction of embarrassments was made more promising still by the recent revelation of the potency of the oil factor. But then there was also, since 1945, the growing awareness of pious Muslims that Western commerce, communications and the simple temptations offered to those rich with oil, were more dangerous to Islam than any earlier (let alone purely military) threat had been. When the descendants of Mehemet Ali (as it were) sent their sons to Harvard and Oxford, they did not, it was feared, acquire only academic instruction there but bad habits as well. This made for strain within Islam.

This was not all that divided Muslims. Sunni and Shi'ite hostility went back cen-turies. In the post-1945 period, the Ba'ath socialist movement which inspired many Muslims and which was nominally entrenched in Iraq, had become anathema to

One of the most obvious effects of the Islamic revolution has been the change in women's clothing. These Iranian women, gathered in Masala Square in Tehran, have exchanged Western dresses for chadors.

the Muslim Brotherhood, which deplored the "godlessness" of both sides even in the Palestinian quarrel. Popular sovereignty was a goal fundamentalists rejected; they sought Islamic control of society in all its aspects, so that, before long, the world began to be used to hearing that Pakistan forbade mixed hockey, that Saudi Arabia punished crime by stoning to death and amputation of limbs, that Oman was building a university in which men and women students were to be segregated during lectures – and much, much more. By 1980, the fundamentalists were powerful enough to secure their goals in some Islamic countries. Even students in a comparatively "westernized" Egypt had already by 1978 been voting for the fundamentalists in their own elections, while some of the girls among them were refusing in medical school to dissect male corpses and demanded a segregated, dual system of instruction.

THE RADICALS' REJECTION OF STATE STRUCTURES

To put so-called "fundamentalist" attitudes in perspective (and at first sight it is not obvious to Western eyes why student "radicals" should happily espouse such obviously reactionary causes), they have to be understood in the context of a long absence within Islam of any state or institutional theory such as that of the West. Even in orthodox hands, and even if it delivered some desirable goods, the state as such is not self-evidently a legitimate authority in Islamic thought – and, on top of that, the very introduction of state structures in Arab lands since the nineteenth century had been in imitation, conscious or unconscious, of the West. Youthful radicalism which had tried and found wanting the politics of left-wing socialism (or what was thought to be that, and was in any case

In 1969, young army officers led by Captain Muammar Gaddafi (b.1942) staged a military coup in Libya, overthrowing King Idris and establishing the Libyan Arabic Republic, an Islamic state with socialist and nationalist leanings. Gaddafi, who promoted himself to the rank of colonel, is accused of supporting terrorist revolutionary groups around the world, and oil-rich Libya has been involved in several clashes with the West.

another Western import) felt that no intrinsic value resided in states or nations; it looked elsewhere, and that, in part, explains the efforts shown first in Libya, and then in Iran, to arrive at new ways of legitimating authority. Whether the age-old Islamic bias against public institutions and towards tribalism and the brotherhood of Islam can be sustained remains to be seen.

The violence of politics in many Arab states frequently exhibits a simple polarization between repressive authoritarianism on the one hand and the fundamentalist wave on the other. In the 1980s both Morocco and Algeria were to find their domestic order thus troubled. The situation was made the more dangerous and explosive by the demography of the Arab lands. The average age of most Islamic societies is said to be between 15 and 18, and they are growing at very fast rates.

There is just too much youthful energy and frustration about for the outlook to be promising for peace.

HOSTAGE-TAKING AND ITS IMPLICATIONS

Soon after the Iran revolution, students in Tehran worked off some of their exasperation by storming the American embassy and seizing diplomats and others as hostages. A startled world suddenly found the Iranian government supporting the students, taking custody of the hostages and endorsing the students' demands for the return of the shah to face trial. President Carter could hardly have faced a more awkward situation at a moment when American policy in the Islamic world was above all preoccupied with Soviet intervention in Afghanistan. A severance of diplomatic relations with Iran and the imposition of economic sanctions were the first responses. Then came an attempted rescue operation, which failed dismally. The unhappy hostages were in the end to be recovered by negotiation (and, in effect, a ransom: the return of Iranian assets in the United States which had been frozen at the time of the revolution), but the humiliation of the Americans was by no means the sole or even the major importance of the episode. Besides its wide policy repercussions, the retention of the hostages was a symbolic moment. It was a shock (registered in a unanimous vote of condemnation at the UN) to the convention that diplomatic envoys should be immune from interference evolved first in Europe and then developed over more than three centuries throughout the civilized world. The Iranian government's action announced that it was not playing by the accepted rules. That was a blatant rejection of Western assumptions which made some in the West wonder what else Islamic revolution might imply.

A ticker-tape parade is held in New York City in 1981 in honour of the American hostages, following their eventual release by Iran after 444 days in captivity.

5 THE END OF AN ERA

Yasser Arafat, leader of the PLO since 1969, is pictured giving a speech before the UN General Assembly in 1974. He spoke passionately about the plight of the Palestinian people and warned, " … today I am holding an olive branch and a freedom-fighter's rifle. Do not let the olive branch fall from my hand … ".

THE HISTORIAN HAS TO DISTIL his account from events which flow uninterruptedly. Now, as never before, those events quickly affect other events the world round and that, too, makes organizing the story of their flow harder. What is more, though they are likely to show greater and faster interaction than in past ages, the current does not run evenly. In one place it hesitates, or is blocked, while elsewhere it rushes on. The phasing of one part of the story does not always match that of other parts. Nevertheless, there are sometimes sweeping waves of change; almost kaleidoscopic rearrangements take place in long-accepted facts and assumptions about very important matters and over wide areas. Suddenly, new mental maps seem to be needed and we talk of turning-points and new eras. The weight of the past seems for a moment to be overcome, or something within it to be breaking out in a new way. This is the sort of thing which justifies historians in attaching special importance to such markers as the Christianizing of the Roman Empire, the destruction of the unity of Christendom in the sixteenth and seventeenth centuries, or the launching of new political ideas on the world by the French Revolution. And now it begins to look as if we may have been experiencing recently the start of just such a big change. Its meaning and even its outlines, at least so far as the world order to which we have grown used is concerned, are still far from clear. But it is a global change at least in political arrangements and assumptions, and (though we must not be too rigid in distinguishing sequences) it has become apparent only since 1985, though more and more dramatically as the end of the decade approached.

Time chart (1974–1990)

	1974–1975 End of the dictatorships in Portugal and Spain	1980 Start of the Iran–Iraq war	1985 Gorbachev becomes general secretary of the Soviet Communist Party	1990 Iraq invades Kuwait Reunification of Germany
1970				**1990**
	1979 USSR invades Afghanistan	1981 Jaruzelski becomes prime minister of Poland	1989 Eastern Europe countries become democracies Tiananmen Square massacre (China)	

THE ISLAMIC MIDDLE EAST

The story can be taken up at the beginning of the 1980s, in a region where great change then seemed imminent but was, in fact, not to follow. This was the Middle East. Though tension there was high in 1980, great disappointment lay ahead for those who hoped for emergence from the Arab–Israeli impasse. For a time, the Iranian revolution looked as if it might transform the rules of the game played hitherto. Ten years later, it was still very difficult to assess in a balanced way what had actually changed, or what was the true significance of Islamic fundamentalism. What had looked for a time like a unified Islamic resurgence can now be seen, at least in part, as one of the recurrent waves of puritanism which have across the centuries helped from time to time to regenerate the faithful. Clearly, too, it owed much to circumstance; Israel's occupation of the third of Islam's Holy Places in Jerusalem had suddenly enhanced the sense of Islamic solidarity. Yet, turning to the Islamic past brought its own difficulties. The attack by Iraq on Iran in 1980 led to a bloody war lasting eight years and costing a million lives. Once more, Islamic peoples were divided along ancient lines: Iraq was Sunnite, Iran Shi'ite.

It soon appeared, too, that although she could irritate and alarm the superpowers (the USSR especially, because of its millions of Muslim subjects), Iran could not thwart them. At the end of 1979, her rulers had to watch helplessly while a Russian army went to Afghanistan to support a puppet Communist régime there against Muslim rebels. This was one reason why they backed terrorists and kidnappers; it was the best (or worst) they could do. Nor, in spite of their success over the American hostages, could the Iranians get back the former shah to face Islamic justice.

THE MIGHT OF THE US

By successfully tweaking the eagle's tail-feathers in the hostage affair, Iran, it is true, humiliated the United States, but in perspective this seems much less significant than it did at the time. In retrospect, a declaration by President Carter in 1980 that the United States regarded the Persian Gulf as an area of vital interest looks more important. It was an early sign of the ending of a dangerously exaggerated mood of American uncertainty and defeatism. A central reality of international politics was about to reassert itself. For all the dramatic changes since the Cuban crisis, the American republic was still in 1980 one of the only two states whose might gave them unquestioned status as (to use an official Soviet definition) "the greatest world powers, without whose participation not a single international problem can be solved". This participation in some instances would be implicit rather than explicit, but it was a fundamental datum of the way the world

The Red Army pulls out of Afghanistan in 1989. The USSR lost 15,000 men in the war against the Islamic fundamentalist Mujahidin guerrillas, in which they remained embroiled for nine difficult years. Three years after the withdrawal of Soviet troops, Afghanistan's Marxist régime was toppled by Muslim forces.

worked. Even a spectacular economic challenge in the Far East and oil blackmail could not affect it, let alone international terrorism.

THE SOVIET UNION'S ARMAMENTS

History has no favourites for long. Though some Americans had been alarmed by the growth in Soviet strength after the Cuban Missile Crisis, there were plentiful signs by the early 1970s that the Soviet rulers were in difficulties. They had to face a truism that Marxism itself proclaimed, that consciousness evolves with material conditions. Among other results of the real but limited rewards Soviet society had given its citizens were two: an evident dissidence, trivial in scale but suggesting a growing demand for greater spiritual freedom, and a less explicit, but real, groundswell of opinion that further material gains should be forthcoming. The Soviet Union nevertheless continued to spend colossal sums on armaments (of the order of a quarter of its GDP in the 1980s). Yet these could hardly suffice, it appeared. To carry even this burden, Western technology, management techniques and, possibly, capital, would be needed. What change might follow on that was debatable, but that there would be change was certain. If nothing else, it seemed unlikely that the huge Soviet military–industrial complex would passively accept a real diminution of its role in the USSR.

MUTUALLY ASSURED DESTRUCTION

Reassuringly, there had grown even stronger by 1980 a compelling tie between the two superpowers. For all the huge effort to give the Soviet Union superior nuclear striking

The Soviet army displays its nuclear missiles in Moscow's Red Square in this May Day parade characteristically used as a show of strength.

Soviet premier Leonid Brezhnev and US president Richard Nixon symbolize the nascent East–West *rapprochement* at arms talks in June 1973.

power over the United States, superiority in these matters at such a level is a rather notional affair. The Americans, with their gift for the arresting slogan, concisely summed up the situation as MAD; that is to say, both countries had the capacity to produce "Mutually Assured Destruction", or, more precisely, a situation in which each of two potential combatants had enough striking power to ensure that even if a surprise attack deprived it of the cream of its weapons, what remained would be sufficient to ensure a reply so appalling as to leave an opponent's cities smoking wildernesses and its armed forces capable of little but attempting to control the terrorized survivors.

This bizarre possibility was a great conservative force. Even though madmen (to put the matter simply) are occasionally to be found in seats of power, Dr Johnson's observation that the knowledge that you are to be hanged wonderfully concentrates the mind is applicable to collectivities threatened with

disaster on this scale: the knowledge that a blunder may be followed by extinction is a great stimulus to prudence. Here may well lie the most fundamental explanation of a new degree of cooperation which began to be shown in the 1970s by the United States and the Soviet Union in spite of specific quarrels. A 1972 treaty on missile limitation was one of its first fruits; it owed something, too, to a new awareness on both sides that science could now monitor infringements of such agreements (not all military research made for an increase of tension). In the following year talks began on further arms limitations while another set of discussions began to explore the possibility of a comprehensive security arrangement in Europe.

EAST–WEST *RAPPROCHEMENT*

In return for the implicit recognition of Europe's post-war frontiers (above all, that

In his years as US president (1981–1989) Ronald Reagan, pictured here in 1980, was extremely vocal in his criticism of the USSR. Although Reagan rejected the idea of détente, he was restrained in the deployment of military force, and American public opinion was against potentially limitless commitments.

between the two Germanies), the Soviet negotiators finally agreed in 1975 at Helsinki to increase economic intercourse between Eastern and Western Europe and to sign a guarantee of human rights and political freedom. The last was, of course, unenforceable. Yet it may well have much outweighed the symbolic gains of frontier recognition to which the Soviet negotiations had attached such importance. Western success over human rights was not only to prove a great encouragement to dissidents in Communist

Europe and Russia, but silently swept aside old restraints on what had been deemed interference in the internal affairs of Communist states. Though very slowly, there began to flow public criticisms which were in the end to help to force change on Communist governments in Eastern Europe. Meanwhile, the flow of trade and investment between the two Europes began almost at once to rise, though slowly. It was the nearest approach so far to a peace treaty ending the Second World War, and it gave the Soviet Union what its leaders most desired, assurance of the territorial security which was one of the major spoils of victory in 1945.

RONALD REAGAN

In spite of the increase in East–West contacts, Americans were very worried about world affairs as 1980, the year of a presidential election, approached. Eighteen years before, the Cuban crisis had shown the world that the United States was top dog. She had then enjoyed superior military strength, the (usually dependable) support of allies, clients and satellites the world round, and the public will to sustain a world diplomatic and military effort while grappling with huge domestic problems. By 1980, many of her citizens felt the world had changed and were unhappy about it. When the new Republican president, Ronald Reagan, took office in 1981, many of his supporters looked back on a decade of what seemed increasing American powerlessness. He inherited an enormous budgetary deficit, disappointment over what looked like recent successful initiatives by the Russians in Africa and Afghanistan, and dismay over what was believed to be the disappearance of the superiority in nuclear weapons the United States had enjoyed in the 1960s.

In the next five years Mr Reagan was to

The assault on the US embassy in Tehran by a group of students in late 1979, and the taking of hostages, humiliated the United States for months. Mass rallies such as this one, in which anti-American demonstrators burn the Stars and Stripes in front of the embassy, shocked the American public.

restore the morale of his countrymen by remarkable (even if often cosmetic) feats of leadership. Symbolically, on the day of his inauguration, the Iranians released their American hostages, the close of a humiliating and frustrating episode (many Americans believed the timing of the release to have been stage-managed by the new administration's supporters). This was by no means the end of the problems American policy faced in the Middle East and the Gulf. Two fundamental difficulties did not go away – the threat posed to international order in that area while Cold War attitudes endured, and the question of Israel. The war between Iran and Iraq was evidence of the danger, many people thought. Soon, the dangerous instability of some Arab countries became more obvious. Ordered government virtually disappeared in the Lebanon, which collapsed into an anarchy disputed by bands of gunmen patronized by the Syrians and Iranians. This gave the

revolutionary wing of the PLO a much more promising base for operation against Israel than in the past. Israel, therefore, took to increasingly violent and expensive military operations on and beyond her northern borders. There followed in the 1980s a heightening of tension and ever more vicious Jewish-Palestinian conflict.

ISLAMIC RADICALIZATION

The United States was not the only great power troubled by these enduring ills. When the Soviet Union sent its soldiers to Afghanistan in 1979 (where they were to stay bogged down for most of the next decade), Iranian and Muslim anger elsewhere was bound to affect Muslims inside the Soviet Union. Some thought this a hopeful sign, believing the growing confusion of the Islamic world might induce caution on the part of the two superpowers, and perhaps lead to less unconditional support for their satellites and allies in the region. This mattered most, of course, to Israel. Meanwhile, the more alarming manifestations and rhetoric of the Iranian revolution made it look for a moment as if a true conflict of civilizations was beginning. Its aggressive puritanism, though, also caused shivers among conservative Arabs and in the oil-rich kingdoms of the Gulf – above all, Saudi Arabia.

There were indeed numerous signs of what looked like spreading sympathy for the radical conservativism of the Iranian revolution in other Islamic countries. Fundamentalists murdered the president of Egypt in 1981. The government of Pakistan continued to proclaim (and impose) its Islamic orthodoxy, and winked at assistance to the anti-Communist Islamic rebels in Afghanistan. (Yet by the end of the decade it had accepted a woman as prime minister, uniquely among Islamic countries, and

even, in 1989, rejoined the British Commonwealth.) North Africa presented more alarming evidence of radical Islamic feeling as the decade drew on. This was less a matter of the bizarre sallies and pronouncements of the excited dictator of Libya (he called upon other oil-producing states to stop supplying the United States while one third of Libyan oil continued to find a market there, and in 1980 briefly "united" his country to Ba'athist Syria) than of political developments further west. Algeria had made a promising start after winning its independence, but by 1980 its economy was flagging, the consensus which had sustained the independence movement was crumbling, and emigration to look for work in Europe seemed the only outlet available for the energies of many of its young men. In the 1990 elections in Algeria, for the first time in any Arab country, an Islamic fundamentalist party won a majority of votes. In the previous year a military coup had brought a military

Members of the Islamic fundamentalist Taliban militia use force to ensure that the inhabitants of Kabul attend Friday prayers at the mosque in 1990. The Taliban have attempted to impose the rigid disciplines of sharia law (the sacred law of Islam) on the areas of Afghanistan under their control.

and militant Islamic fundamentalist régime to power in the Sudan which at once suppressed the few remaining civic freedoms of the people of that unhappy land.

THE WEAK POINTS OF FUNDAMENTALISM

For all the attractions of Islamic radicalization, there were plentiful signs by 1990 that more moderate and conservative Arab politicians had been antagonized, and that indigenous opposition to the fundamentalists was significant and sometimes effective. It remains hard to believe that sufficient leverage is available to the would-be revolutionaries, even after setting aside both such political realities and deeper questions about the feasibility of successful Islamic revolution when so many of its would-be supporters sought, unknowingly, to realize goals of power and modernization systematically incompatible with Islamic teaching and custom. Libya could destabilize other African countries and arm Irish terrorists, but achieved little else. Because of preoccupations of changing circumstances elsewhere, the old Soviet-American rivalry was decreasingly available for exploitation. All that was left for the fundamentalists to look to were two potentially rich countries, Iraq and Iran, and for most of the 1980s they were fatally entangled in a costly struggle with one another.

There was also growing evidence that the ruler of Iraq, patronized by the Americans and the major trouble-maker of the Middle East, was only tactically and pragmatically a supporter of Islam. Saddam Hussein was a Muslim by upbringing, but led a formally secular Ba'athist régime actually based on patronage, family and the self-interest of soldiers. He sought power, and technological

Saddam Hussein (b.1937) became president of Iraq in 1979. In 1980 he declared war on Iran, with the aim of liquidating the Iranian revolution: the conflict lasted until 1988. While final peace negotiations were still under way Hussein invaded Kuwait in August 1990. This provoked the brief Gulf War, involving a multinational UN force, in which Iraq was defeated.

modernization as a way to it, and there is no evidence that the welfare of the Iraqi people ever concerned him. When he launched his war on Iran, the prolongation of the struggle and evidence of its costs were greeted with relief by other Arab states – notably the other oil-producers of the Gulf – because it appeared at the same time to pin down both a dangerous bandit and the Iranian revolutionaries whom they feared. It was, however, less pleasing to them that the Gulf War distracted attention from the Palestinian question and unquestionably strengthened Israel's hand in dealing with the PLO.

THE PALESTINIAN *INTIFADA*

During nearly a decade of alarums and excursions in the Gulf, some of which raised the spectre of further interference with Western oil supplies, incidents seemed at times to threaten a widening of armed conflict, notably between Iran and the United States. Meanwhile, events in the Levant embittered the stalemate there. Israel's annexation of the Golan Heights, her vigorous operations in Lebanon against Palestinian guerrilla bands and their patrons, and her government's encouragement of further Jewish immigration (notably from the USSR) all helped to buttress her against the day when she might once again face united Arab armies. At the end of 1987, though, there came the first outbreaks of violence among Palestinians in the Israeli-occupied territories. They persisted and grew into an enduring insurrection, the *intifada*. The PLO, though it won further international sympathy by officially recognizing Israel's own right to exist was none the less in a disadvantaged position in 1989, when the Iran–Iraq war finally ended. In the following year the Ayatollah Khomeini died and there were signs that his successor might be less adventurous in support of both the Palestinian and the fundamentalist Islamic cause.

THE GULF WAR

During the Iran–Iraq war, the United States had favoured Iraq, seeing Iran as a danger. This was in part because of American overestimation of the fundamentalist threat. When, nevertheless, the Americans found themselves at last face-to-face at war in the Gulf with a declared enemy, it was with the Iraqis, not the Iranians. In 1990, after making a generous peace with Iran, Hussein took up an old border dispute with the sheikdom of Kuwait. He had also quarrelled with its ruler over oil quotas and prices. It is not easy to believe in the reality of these grievances; whatever they may have meant symbolically to Hussein himself, what seems to have moved him most was a simple determination to seize the immense oil wealth of Kuwait.

Iraqi anti-aircraft fire is used against American and allied bombers attacking Baghdad in January 1991. The Gulf War, called "the mother of all battles" by Saddam Hussein, had more than a human cost – it also caused severe environmental damage. The water in the region was polluted by millions of litres of spilt oil and the Iraqi leader ordered his troops to set fire to the oil wells.

During the summer of 1990, his threats increased. Then, on 2 August, the armies of Iraq invaded Kuwait, and in a few hours subdued it.

There followed a remarkable mobilization of world opinion against Iraq in the UN. Hussein sought to play both the Islamic and the Arab cards by confusing the pursuit of his own predatory ambitions with Arab hatred for Israel. Except in the streets of Middle Eastern cities, where there were many demonstrations in his favour, they proved to be cards of very low value. Only the PLO and Jordan spoke up for him. No doubt to his shocked surprise, Saudi Arabia, Syria and Egypt, on the other hand, actually became improbable partners in the alliance which rapidly formed against him. Almost equally surprising to him must have been the acquiescence of the USSR in what followed. Finally, and most startlingly of all, the United Nations Security Council produced (with overwhelming majorities) a series of

resolutions condemning Iraq's actions and, finally, authorizing the use of force against her to ensure the liberation of Kuwait. Once again, a much-feared second oil crisis did not follow.

THE MIDDLE EAST AFTER THE GULF WAR

Huge forces were assembled in Saudi Arabia under American command. On 16 January, 1991 they went into action. Within a month Iraq gave in and withdrew, after suffering considerable loss (allied losses were by comparison insignificant). It is too soon to weigh all the consequences of that humiliation, though it did not obviously threaten Hussein's survival. It was not the turning-point in the Middle East which so many longed for. Yet, in spite of Hussein's attempts to inspire an anti-Israel Islamic crusade, he had not found takers; it was no turning-point

An American soldier passes dead Iraqi troops during the Gulf War. It had quickly become clear that the Iraqi army stood no chance of victory against the United Nations forces of around half a million drawn from several nations.

for Arab revolutionaries, either. The greater losers were the PLO. Israel was the greatest gainer. Arab military success at her expense was inconceivable for the near future. Yet at the end of one more war of the Ottoman succession, the Israel–Arab problem was still there. Syria and Iran had already before the Kuwait crisis begun to show signs that, for their own reasons, they intended to make attempts to get a negotiated settlement, but whether one would emerge was another matter. For the United States, it was clearly more of a priority than ever to get one and that encouraged hopes that Israel might, at last, show less intransigence. At the least, the alarming spectre of a radical and fundamentalist pan-Islamic movement had been dissipated. For all the unrest and discontent with which Islamic countries faced the West, there was virtually no sign that their resentments could yet be coordinated in an effective response, and less than ever that they could do without the subtly corrosive means of modernization which the West offered. Almost incidentally, too, crisis in the Gulf appeared to reveal that the oil weapon had lost much of its power to damage the developed world. It was against this background that American diplomacy was at last success-

ful in 1991 in persuading Arabs and Jews to take part in a conference on the Middle East. With great effort, preliminary contacts were developed into informal discussion, and then into negotiation, which at Oslo in 1993 produced agreements in principle between the Israeli government and the PLO. These appeared at last to have given the Palestinian state the first significant diplomatic gains it had made in its history and were intended to inaugurate five years of measured management of the details of a settlement. Unhappily, the continuing establishment of new Jewish settlements in the areas occupied by the Israeli forces soon poisoned the atmosphere again. It also gave rise to new bitterness in Israel's own politics, a fact shockingly marked in 1996 when her prime minister was assassinated by a Zionist fanatic.

MIKHAIL GORBACHEV

The great transformations of the 1980s had, in the end, turned out to have changed very little in the Middle East. They bore upon events there only because they shaped what the USA and USSR did there. In 1979–80, the American presidential election campaign had been deliberately fought so as to play on the public's fears of the Soviet Union. Unsurprisingly, this re-awoke animosity at the official level; the conservative leaders of the Soviet Union showed renewed suspicion of the trend of United States policy. It seemed likely that promising steps towards disarmament might be swept aside – or even worse. In the event, the American administration showed a remarkable pragmatism in foreign affairs, while, on the Soviet side, internal change was to open the way to greater flexibility.

One crucial event was the death, in November 1982, of Leonid Brezhnev,

In the 1970s, the USSR opened its borders to foreign businesses and scenes such as this queue of people outside a McDonald's fast-food restaurant in Moscow in 1990 became increasingly common.

Mikhail Gorbachev

In March 1985, Mikhail Gorbachev (b.1931) became secretary-general of the Soviet Communist Party. At the 27th Party Congress in February 1986, Gorbachev announced the revision of some of the state policies that were increasingly being questioned by the Soviet people. Gorbachev seemed to want to construct a constitutional democratic state based on upholding the law and respect for civil liberties. This implied the separation of the Party from the State and the removal of the effective centre of government from the Party to the State. This in turn meant the end of the one-party system. In foreign affairs, Gorbachev launched what has been called the "détente

offensive", signing arms limitations treaties in an attempt to reduce the huge drain the Soviet military put on the economy.

Mikhail Gorbachev is pictured during the 1990 meeting of the Soviet Council, the year before his resignation.

Khrushchev's successor and for eighteen years general secretary of the Party. His immediate replacement (the head of the KGB) soon died and a septuagenarian whose own death followed even more quickly succeeded him before there came to the office of general secretary in 1985 the youngest member of the Politburo, Mr Mikhail Gorbachev. He was fifty-four. Virtually the whole of his political experience had been of the post-Stalin era. His impact upon his country's, and the world's, history cannot yet be properly assessed. His personal motivation and the conjunction of forces which propelled him to the succession remains unclear. The KGB, presumably, did not oppose his promotion, and his first acts and speeches were orthodox (although he had already, in the previous year, made an impression on the British prime minister as "someone with whom business could be done"). He soon articulated a new

political tone. The word "communism" was heard less in his speeches and "socialism" was re-interpreted to exclude egalitarianism (though from time to time he reminded his colleagues that he *was* a Communist). For want of a better term, his aim was seen as liberalization, which was an inadequate Western attempt to sum up two Russian words he used a great deal: *glasnost* (openness) and *perestroika* (restructuring). The implications of the new course were to be profound and dramatic, and for the remainder of the decade Mr Gorbachev was to grapple with them. In the end there became clear his recognition that the Soviet economy could no longer provide its former military might, sustain its commitments to allies abroad, improve (however slowly) living standards at home, and assure self-generated technological innovation without radical modernization. The implications of that were vast.

ARMS LIMITATION TALKS

Mr Reagan drew the first dividends on Mr Gorbachev's arrival in power. In the sphere of foreign affairs, the Soviet leader's new course soon became clear in their meetings. Discussion of arms reduction was renewed. Agreements were reached on other issues, and this was made easier by the decision of the Soviet leadership in 1989 to withdraw their forces from Afghanistan. In America's domestic politics, a huge budgetary deficit, and a flagging economy which would under most presidents have produced political uproar were for years virtually lost to sight in the euphoria produced by a seeming transformation of the international scene. The alarm and fear with which the "evil empire" (as Mr Reagan had termed it) of the Soviet Union was regarded by many Americans began to evaporate. Optimism and confidence grew as the USSR showed signs of growing division and difficulty in reforming its affairs. What was more, Americans had been promised wonders by their government in the shape of new defensive measures in outer space. Though thousands of scientists said the project was unrealistic, the Soviet government

Gorbachev and Reagan sign the Treaty of Washington in December 1988, ending the stockpiling of intermediate-range nuclear missiles. This represented the beginning of the end of the arms race and was also influential in moving several regional conflicts towards viable solutions.

The American bombing raids on Tripoli, Libya, in 1986 failed to eliminate Gaddafi, but killed and maimed a number of civilians. Here, Libyan soldiers shouting anti-American slogans surround the body of an old man who was killed in a US air raid.

could not face the costs of competing with that. Americans were heartened, too, in 1986 when American bombers were launched from England on a punitive mission against Libya, whose unbalanced ruler had been supporting anti-American terrorists (significantly, the Soviet Union expressed less concern about this than did many West Europeans). The president was less successful, though, in convincing many of his countrymen that more enthusiastic assertions of American's interests in Central America were truly in their interests. But he survived as a remarkably popular figure; only after he had left office did it begin to dawn that for most Americans the decade had been one in which they had got poorer.

In 1987, the fruits of negotiation on arms control were gathered in an agreement over intermediate-range nuclear missiles. In spite of so many shocks and its erosion by the emergence of new foci of power, the nuclear balance had held long enough for the first stand-downs by the superpowers. They had shown they could still manage their conflicts and the world's crises without all-out war, after all. They at least, if not other countries seeking to acquire nuclear weapons, appeared to have recognized that nuclear war, if it came, held out the prospect of virtual extinction for humanity, and were slowly beginning to do something about it. In 1991 there were further dramatic developments as the USA and USSR agreed to major reductions in existing weapons stocks.

EASTERN EUROPE

SUCH A HUGE CHANGE in the international scene as the superpower stand-down cannot be disentangled from its many consequences for other nations. They have to be artificially separated to be expounded, but one could not have occurred without the other. At the end of 1980 there had been little reason to believe that the peoples of Eastern Europe and the Soviet Union were about to enter a new phase of their destiny, a decade bringing changes unmatched since the 1940s. All that then could be seen was the growing difficulty of European Communist countries in maintaining even the modest growth rates they attained. Comparison with the market economies of the non-Communist world had become more and more unfavourable to them. Yet this hardly suggested any challenge to the verdicts of 1952, 1956 and 1968: in 1980 Soviet power seemed to hold Eastern Europe as firmly as ever in its grip.

ECONOMIC STAGNATION

What had been, in a measure, lost to sight within the carapace provided by the Warsaw Pact was social and political change which had been going on for thirty years (and more, if one counts the great unwilled changes of the Second World War and its aftermath). At first sight, the outcome of a long experiment with a particular model of development had been a remarkable uniformity. In each Communist-ruled country, the Party was supreme; careerists built their lives round it as, in earlier centuries, men on the make clustered about courts and patrons. In each (and above all in the USSR itself) there was also an unspeakable and unexaminable past which could not be mourned or deplored, whose weight overhung and corrupted intellectual life and political discussion, so far as there was any. As for the East European economies,

Pictured is the National Textile Industry building in Sibernik in the former Yugoslavia. Before the outbreak of civil war, the country had a centrally planned economy, with around a quarter of the workforce employed in state-run manufacturing industries.

When Alexander Dubcek (1921–1992) became first secretary of the Czechoslovakian Communist Party in January 1968, he immediately began to implement liberalizing reforms, for which he received widespread public support. Observers in Moscow, however, quickly lost their patience with the "Prague Spring"; in August they sent 650,000 Warsaw Pact troops to bring the country back into line. Here, a young man stands on one of the invading tanks, brandishing the Czech flag in defiance.

investment in heavy industrial and capital goods had produced a surge of early growth (in some of them more vigorous than in others) and then an international system of trading arrangements with other Communist countries, dominated by the USSR and rigidified by aspirations to central planning. Increasingly and obviously, a growing thirst for consumer goods could not be met; commodities taken for granted in Western Europe remained luxuries in the East European countries, cut off as they were from the advantages of international economic specialization. On the land, private ownership had been much reduced by the middle of the 1950s, usually to be replaced by a mixture of cooperatives and state farms, though, within this broadly uniform picture, different patterns had later emerged. In Poland, for instance, peasants were already moving back into smallholdings by 1960; eventually, something like four-fifths of Polish farmland was to return to private ownership even under Communist

government. Output remained low; in most East European countries agricultural yields were only from half to three-quarters those of the European Community. By the 1980s all of them, in varying degrees, were in a state of economic crisis with the possible exception only of the GDR. Even there, per capita GDP stood at only $9,300 a year in 1988, against $19,500 in the Federal Republic.

THE BREZHNEV DOCTRINE

What had come to be called the "Brezhnev doctrine" (after a speech that a functionary made in Warsaw in 1968) said that developments within Eastern bloc countries might require – as in Czechoslovakia that year – direct intervention to safeguard the interests of the USSR and its allies against any attempts to turn socialist economies back towards capitalism. Yet Brezhnev had also been interested in pursuing détente and it was not unreasonable to interpret his doctrine as a recognition of the possible dangers presented to international stability by breakaway developments in Communist Europe, and a way of limiting them by drawing clearer lines. Since then, internal change in Western countries, steadily growing more prosperous, and with memories of the late 1940s and the seeming possibility of subversion far behind them, had not increased East–West tension. By 1980, after revolutionary changes in Spain and Portugal, not a dictatorship survived west of the Trieste–Stettin line and democracy was everywhere triumphant. For thirty years, the only risings by industrial workers against their political masters had been in East Germany, Hungary, Poland and Czechoslovakia – all Communist countries (conspicuously, when Paris was in uproar in 1968, and student riots destroyed the prestige of de Gaulle's government, the Parisian working class had done nothing).

After 1970, and even more after the Helsinki agreement of 1975, as awareness of contrasts with Western Europe grew in the Eastern bloc, dissident groups emerged, survived and even strengthened their positions, in spite of severe repression. Gradually, too, a few officials or economic specialists, and even some Party members, began to show signs of scepticism about the effects of detailed centralized planning and there was increasing discussion of the advantages of utilizing market mechanisms. The key to stability in the East, nevertheless, remained the Soviet army. There was no reason to believe that fundamental change was possible in any of the Warsaw Pact countries if the Brezhnev doctrine held, and continued to provide support to governments subservient to the USSR.

POLAND AND SOLIDARITY

The first clear sign that change might be possible in the Soviet bloc came in the early

When John Paul II (born in 1920) – the first non-Italian pope since 1523 – visited Poland in June 1979 his tacit expression of the Church's opposition to Communism boosted the strength of the Polish Solidarity movement. Here, the pontiff is pictured during a 1991 visit with Lech Walesa, the Solidarity leader who had become president of Poland at the end of the previous year.

Solidarity leader Lech Walesa addresses striking Polish workers at the Lenin Shipyard in Gdansk in 1980.

1980s, in Poland. The Polish nation had retained, to a remarkable degree (but not for the first time in its history), its collective integrity by following its priests and not its rulers. The Roman Catholic Church had an enduring hold on the affections and minds of most Poles as the embodiment of the nation, and was often to speak for them – all the more convincingly when a Polish pope had been enthroned. It did so on behalf of workers who protested in the 1970s against economic policy, and condemned their ill-treatment. This, together with the worsening of economic conditions, was the background to 1980, a year of crisis for Poland. A series of strikes then came to a head in an epic struggle in the Gdansk shipyard. From them emerged a new and spontaneously organized federation of trades unions, "Solidarity". It added political demands to the economic goals of the strikers, among them one for free and independent trades unions. Solidarity's leader was a remarkable, often-imprisoned, electrical union leader, Lech Walesa, a devout

Catholic, closely in touch with the Polish hierarchy. The shipyard gates were decorated with a picture of the pope and open-air masses were held by the strikers.

The world was surprised to see, soon, a shaken Polish government, troubled as strikes spread, making historic concessions. The crucial step was that Solidarity was recognized as an independent, self-governing trade union. Symbolically, regular broadcasting of the Catholic mass on Sundays was also conceded. But disorder did not cease, and with the winter, the atmosphere of crisis deepened. Threats were heard from Poland's neighbours of possible intervention; forty Soviet divisions were said to be ready in the GDR and on the Russian frontier. But the dog did not bark in the night; the Soviet army did not move and was not ordered by Brezhnev to do so, nor by his successors in the turbulent years which followed. It was the first sign of changes in Moscow which were the necessary premise of what was to follow in Eastern Europe in the next ten years.

LECH WALESA

In 1981, tension continued to rise in Poland, the economic situation worsened, but Walesa strove to avert provocation. On five occasions the Russian commander of the Warsaw Pact forces came to Warsaw. On the last occasion, the Solidarity radicals broke away from Walesa's control and called for a general strike if emergency powers were taken by the government. On 13 December, martial law was declared. There followed fierce repression (opposition may have cost hundreds of lives). But the Polish military's action may also have helped to make Russian invasion unnecessary. Solidarity went underground, to begin seven years of struggle, during which it became more and more evident that the military government could neither prevent further economic deterioration, nor enlist the support of the "real" Poland, the society alienated from Communism, for the régime. A moral revolution was taking place. As one Western observer put it, Poles began to behave "as if they lived in a free country"; clandestine organization and publication, strikes and demonstrations, and continuing ecclesiastical condemnation of the régime sustained what was at times an atmosphere of civil war.

Although after a few months the government cautiously abandoned formal martial law, it still continued to deploy a varied repertoire of overt and undercover repression. Meanwhile, the economy declined further, Western countries offered no help and little sympathy, and, after 1985, the change in Moscow began to produce its effects. Yet the climax came only in 1989, for Poland her greatest year since 1945, as it was for other countries, too, thanks to her example. It opened with the régime's acceptance that other political parties and organizations, including Solidarity, had to share in the political process. As a first step to true political

pluralism, elections were held in June in which some seats were freely contested. Solidarity swept the board in them. Soon the new parliament denounced the German-Soviet agreement of August 1939, condemned the 1968 invasion of Czechoslovakia, and set up investigations into political murders committed since 1981.

THE REPUBLIC OF POLAND

In August 1989 Walesa announced that Solidarity would support a coalition government; the Communist diehards were told by Mr Gorbachev that this would be justifiable (and some Soviet military units had already left the country). In September a coalition dominated by Solidarity and led by the first non-Communist prime minister since 1945 took office as the government of Poland. Western economic aid was soon promised. By Christmas the Polish People's Republic had passed from history and,

L ech Walesa walks to Warsaw's cathedral on the day of his inauguration as the president of Poland in December 1990.

once again, the historic republic of Poland had risen from its grave.

Poland led Eastern Europe to freedom. The importance of events there had quickly been perceived in other Communist countries, whose leaders were much alarmed. In varying degree, too, all Eastern Europe was exposed to the new factor of a steadily increasing flow of information about non-Communist countries, above all, through television (which was especially marked in the GDR). More freedom of movement, more access to foreign books and newspapers had imperceptibly advanced the process of criticism there as in Poland. In spite of some ludicrous attempts to go on controlling information (Romania still required that typewriters be registered with the state authorities), a change in consciousness was under way.

ECONOMIC DECLINE IN THE SOVIET UNION

Mr Gorbachev had come to power during the early stages of the changes in Communist countries. Five years later, it was clear that his assumption of office had released revolutionary institutional change in the Soviet Union too, first, as power was taken from the Party, and then as the opportunities so provided were seized by newly emerging opposition forces, above all in republics of the Union which began to claim greater or lesser degrees of autonomy. Before long, it began to look as if he might be undermining his own authority. Paradoxically, too, and alarmingly, the economic picture looked worse and worse. It became clear that a transition to a market economy, whether slow or rapid, was likely to impose far greater hardship on many – perhaps most – Soviet citizens than had been envisaged. By 1989 it was clear that the Soviet economy was out of control and running down. As always before in Russian history, modernization had been launched from the centre and flowed out to the periphery through authoritarian structures. But that was precisely what could not now be relied upon to happen, first because of the resistance of the *nomenklatura* and the administration of the command economy, and then, at the end of the decade, because of the visibly and rapidly crumbling power of the centre.

By 1990 much more information was available to the rest of the world about the true state of the Soviet Union and its people's attitudes than ever before. Not only were there many overt signs of popular feeling, but glasnost had brought to the Soviet Union its first surveys of public opinion through polls. Some rough-and-ready judgments could be made: the discrediting of the Party and *nomenklatura* was profound, even if it had not by 1990 gone so far as in some other Warsaw Pact countries (more surprisingly, the long unprotesting Orthodox Church appeared to have retained more respect and authority than other institutions of the Marxist-Leninist *ancien régime*).

The Soviet economy had collapsed by the winter of 1990–1991. Food shortages struck in the cities. Here, Muscovites queue for the few available products in a Russian supermarket in which most of the shelves are bare. Ration books were eventually introduced in some areas, but they had to be withdrawn owing to a lack of supplies.

As the economy of the Soviet Union collapsed, food shortages brought desperation to the cities, particularly in winter. Here, a pensioner picks over the contents of a rubbish dump on the outskirts of Moscow in search of food.

The Soviet Union and its successors

The USSR made its last territorial acquisitions during the Second World War, when it annexed territories along its western borders, including the three Baltic states. From 1945, the integrity of the 15 republics that made up the USSR was threatened only by minor border conflicts with China. Following the collapse of Communism in 1991, the former Soviet republics declared their independence. All except the Baltic states are now members of the Commonwealth of Independent States.

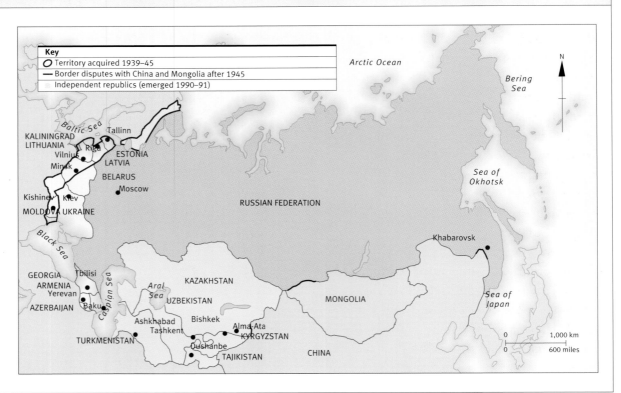

Key
○ Territory acquired 1939–45
— Border disputes with China and Mongolia after 1945
  Independent republics (emerged 1990–91)

THE COLLAPSE OF THE SOVIET UNION

It was clear that economic failure everywhere hung like a cloud over any liberalizing of political processes. Soviet citizens as well as foreign observers began to talk by 1989 of the possibility of civil war. The thawing of the iron grip of the past had revealed the power of nationalist and regional sentiment when excited by economic collapse and opportunity. After seventy years of efforts to make Soviet citizens, the USSR was revealed to be a collection of peoples as distinct as ever, organized in fifteen republics, some of which (above all the three Baltic republics of Latvia, Estonia and Lithuania) were quick to show dissatisfaction with their lot and, in the end, were to lead the way to political change. Azerbaijan and Soviet Armenia posed problems which were complicated by the shadow of Islamic unrest which hung over the whole Union. To make matters worse, some believed there was a danger of a military coup; commanders who were as discontented by the Soviet failure in Afghanistan as some American soldiers had been by withdrawal from Vietnam were talked about as potential Bonapartes – a danger long flourished as a bogey of Bolshevik mythology.

The signs of disintegration multiplied, although Mr Gorbachev succeeded in clinging to office and, indeed, in obtaining formal enhancements of his nominal powers. (But this had the disadvantage of focusing responsibility for failure, too.) One dramatic moment came in March 1990, when a declaration of the Lithuanian parliament declared the annexation of 1939 invalid and reasserted Lithuania's independence, though this was followed by complicated negotiation to avoid provoking the armed suppression of the revived republic by Soviet forces. Latvia and Estonia also claimed their independence, though in slightly different terms. The upshot was that Mr Gorbachev did not seek to revoke the fact of secession, but in return won agreements that the other Baltic republics should guarantee the continued existence of certain practical services to the USSR. Yet this proved to be the beginning of the end for Mr Gorbachev. A period of increasingly rapid manoeuvring between reforming and conservative groups, allying himself first to one and then, to redress the balance, to the other led by the end of 1990, to the compromise of the previous summer already looking out of date and unworkable. Connivance at repressive action by the soldiers and KGB in Vilnius and Riga early in the new year did not stem the tide. Parliaments in nine of the Soviet republics had already by then either declared they were sovereign or had asserted a substantial degree of independence from the

Union government. Some of them had made local languages official; and some had transferred Soviet ministries and economic agencies to local control. The Russian republic – the most important – set out to run its own economy separately from that of the Union. The Ukrainian republic proposed to set up its own army. In March, elections led Mr Gorbachev once more back to the path of reform and a search for a new Union treaty which could preserve some central role for the state. The world looked on, bemused.

THE BERLIN WALL IS DEMOLISHED

The Polish example combined with growing realization that after 1986 an increasingly divided and paralysed USSR would not (perhaps could not) intervene to uphold its creatures in the Communist Party bureaucracies of the other Warsaw Pact countries and

East Berliners clamber on the defunct Berlin Wall in November 1989. The collapse of the Communist German Democratic Republic and German reunification were to follow the bringing down of the wall – events that had been unthinkable less than a decade earlier.

so determine what happened in them after 1986. The Hungarians had moved almost as rapidly in economic liberalization as the Poles, even before overt political change, but their most important contribution to the dissolution of Communist Europe came in August 1989. Germans from the GDR were then allowed to enter Hungary freely as tourists, though their purpose was known to be to present themselves to the embassy and consulates of the Federal Republic for asylum. A complete opening of Hungary's frontiers came in September (when Czechoslovakia followed suit) and a flow became a flood. In three days 12,000 East Germans crossed from these countries to the West. The Soviet authorities remarked that this was "unusual". For the GDR it was the beginning of the end. On the eve of the carefully-planned and much-vaunted celebration of forty years' "success" as a socialist country, and during a visit by Mr Gorbachev (who, to the dismay of the German Communists, appeared to urge the East Germans to seize their chance), riot police had to battle with anti-government demonstrators on the streets of East Berlin. The government and Party threw out their leader, but this was not enough. November opened with huge demonstrations in many cities against a régime whose corruption was becoming evident; on 9 November came the greatest symbolic act of all, the breaching of the Berlin Wall. The East German Politburo caved in and the demolition of the rest of the wall followed.

FREE ELECTIONS

More than anywhere else, events in the GDR showed that even in the most advanced Communist countries there had been a massive

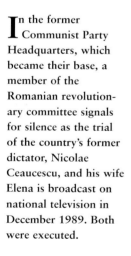

In the former Communist Party Headquarters, which became their base, a member of the Romanian revolutionary committee signals for silence as the trial of the country's former dictator, Nicolae Ceaucescu, and his wife Elena is broadcast on national television in December 1989. Both were executed.

THE END OF AN ERA

alienation of popular feeling from the régime. Nineteen eighty-nine had brought it to a head. All over Eastern Europe, it was suddenly clear that Communist governments had no legitimacy in the eyes of their subjects, who either rose against them or turned their backs and let them fall down. The institutional expression of this alienation was everywhere a demand for free elections, with opposition parties freely campaigning. The Poles had followed their own partially free elections, in which some seats were still reserved to supporters of the existing régime, with the preparation of a new constitution; in 1990, Lech Walesa became president. A few months earlier, Hungary had elected a parliament from which emerged a non-Communist government. Soviet soldiers began to withdraw from the country. In June 1990, Czechoslovakian elections produced a free government and it was soon agreed that the country was to be evacuated of Soviet forces by May 1991. In none of these countries did the former Communist politicians get more than 16 per cent of the vote. Free election in Bulgaria was less decisive: there, the contest was won by Communist Party members turned reformers and calling themselves socialists.

GERMAN REUNIFICATION

In two countries, events turned out differently. Romania underwent a violent revolution (ending in the killing of its former Communist dictator) after a rising in December 1989 which revealed uncertainties about the way ahead and internal divisions ominously foreshadowing further strife. By June 1990 a government some believed still to be heavily influenced by former Communists had turned on some of its former supporters, now critics, and crushed student protest with the aid of vigilante squads of miners at some

cost in lives and in disapproval abroad. The GDR was the other country where events took a special turn. It was bound to be a special case, because the question of political change was inescapably bound up with the question of German reunification. The breaching of the wall revealed that not only was there no political will to support Communism, there was no will to support the GDR either. A general election there in March 1990 gave a majority of seats (and a 48 per cent vote) to a coalition dominated by the Christian Democrat party – the ruling party of the western German Federal Republic. Unity was no longer in doubt; only the procedure and timetable remained to be settled.

In July the two Germanies joined in a monetary, economic and social union. In October they united, the former territories of the GDR becoming provinces of the Federal Republic. The change was momentous, but no serious alarm was openly expressed, even in Moscow, and Mr Gorbachev's acquiescence was his second great service to the German nation. Yet alarm there must have been in the USSR. The new Germany would

In the East German town of Magdeburg, a mixed crowd turns out to listen to the chancellor of the FDR Helmut Kohl make a speech during his election campaign in early 1990.

Soldiers from a British battalion of the United Nations peace-keeping forces are seen on patrol in Bosnia during the civil war in the former Yugoslavia.

be the greatest European power to the west. Russian power was now in eclipse as it had not been since 1918. The reward for Mr Gorbachev was a treaty with the new Germany promising economic help with Soviet modernization. It might also be said, by way of reassurance to those who remembered 1941–5, that the new German state was not just an older Germany revived. Germany was now shorn of the old east German lands (had, indeed, formally renounced them) and was not dominated by Prussia as both Bismarck's Reich and the Weimar Republic had been. More reassuring still (and of importance to West Europeans who felt misgivings), the Federal Republic was a federal and constitutional state seemingly assured of economic success, with nearly forty years' experience of democratic politics to build on, and embedded in the structures of the EC and NATO. She was given the benefit of the doubt by West Europeans with long memories, at least for the time being.

THE DISINTEGRATION OF YUGOSLAVIA

At the end of 1990, the condition of what had once seemed the almost monolithic East European bloc already defied generalization or brief description. As former Communist countries (Czechoslovakia, Poland, Hungary) applied to join the EC, or got ready to do so (Bulgaria), some observers speculated about a potentially wider degree of European unity than ever before. More cautious judgments were made by those who noted the virulent emergence of new – or re-emergence of old – national and communal division to plague the new East. Above all, over the whole area there gathered the storm-clouds of economic failure and the turbulence they might bring. Liberation might have come, but it had come

to peoples and societies of very different levels of sophistication and development, and with very different historical origins. Prediction was clearly unwise.

How unwise became clear in 1991. In that year, a jolt was given to optimism over the prospects of peaceful change when two of the constituent republics of Yugoslavia announced their decision to separate from the federal state. Their decision was shaped by deep-rooted national animosities which had for years been increasingly evident in the Serb-dominated republic. In August, sporadic fighting by both air and ground forces began between Serbs and Croats. Precedents for intervention by outsiders did not ever seem promising – though different views were held by different EC countries – and such a prospect became even less attractive when the USSR in July uttered a warning about the dangers of spreading local conflict to the international level. By the end of the year Macedonia, Bosnia-Herzegovina and Slovenia had all had joined Croatia in declaring themselves independent of the Yugoslav federal republic. Unhappily, history had left to that region a particularly poisoned legacy of old ethnic and religious hatreds, and too confused a pattern of settlement between distinct communities for any dissolution of the old order to be easily or swiftly available. Instead a period of savage struggles followed above all in Bosnia, marked by expulsions, massacres and terror, as Serbs, Bosnian Serbs and Bosnian Muslims strove to disentangle their claims to villages and towns, and even to quarters of the same towns. Fighting was in the end contained openly by intervention by NATO forces and the virtual imposition of partition from the outside in 1995. Formal peace, though, did not conceal the likelihood that before long other aspiring national groups would be likely to disrupt things again.

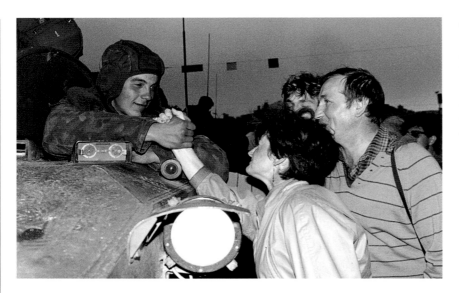

Demonstrators shake hands with a tank driver during the failed coup of August 1991 in Moscow. Gorbachev's opponents took advantage of his absence from the capital to stage their coup. They believed they would be welcomed by the masses, who would applaud a "return to normality", but they had badly misjudged the public mood and only a small minority supported the attempt.

determined replacement of Union officialdom at all levels, the redefinition of roles for the KGB and a redistribution of control over it between the Union and the republics. The most striking change of all was the demolition of the Communist Party of the Soviet Union, which began almost at once. Almost bloodlessly, at least to begin with, it appeared, the huge creation which had grown out of the Bolshevik coup of 1917 was coming to an end. There seemed at first good grounds for rejoicing over that, though it was not clear that nothing but good would follow.

THE RUSSIAN COUP OF 1991

The Soviet warning was the last diplomatic *démarche* of the régime. It was soon eclipsed by a much more momentous event. On 19 August a still mysterious attempt was made by conservatives to set aside Mr Gorbachev by *coup d'état*. It failed, and three days later he was again in occupation of the presidency. Nonetheless, his position was not the same; continual changes of side in a search for compromise had ruined his political credibility. He had clung too long to the Party and the Union; Soviet politics had taken a further lurch forward. To many it seemed as if it was toward disintegration. The circumstances of the coup had given an opportunity which he seized to Mr Boris Yeltsin, the leader of the Russian republic, the largest in the Union. The army, the only conceivable threat to his supporters, did not move against him. He now appeared both as the strong man of the Soviet scene without whose concurrence nothing could be done, and as a possible standard-bearer for a Russian chauvinism which might threaten other republics. While foreign observers waited to understand, the purging of those who had supported or acquiesced in the coup was developed into a

THE CIS IS FORMED

The fact that the end of Communism might bring mixed blessings became clearer as the year came to an end. With the decision to abandon price controls in the Russian republic in the near future, it seemed likely that not only inflation unparalleled since the earliest days of the Soviet system, but perhaps starvation, too, would soon face millions of Russians. In another republic, Georgia, fighting had already broken out between the supporters of the president elected after the first free elections there and the discontented opposition. Dwarfing all such facts, though, was the end of the great Soviet Union itself. The giant superpower which had emerged from the bloody experiments of the Bolshevik revolution to be, almost to the end, for nearly seventy years the hope of revolutionaries around the world, and the generator of military strength that had fought and won the greatest land campaigns in history, dissolved suddenly and helplessly into a set of successor states. The last of the great European multinational empires had gone. Russian, Ukrainian and Belorussian leaders met at Minsk on 8 December and announced the end of the Soviet Union and the establishment

Georgia, the birthplace of Stalin, became independent from the Soviet Union on 9 April, 1991. In the 1990s attempts by ethnic groups in Abkhazia and South Ossetia to secede from Georgia resulted in bloody civil wars. Here, women from South Ossetia carry photographs of their husbands and sons who they claim were shot by Georgian soldiers.

of a new "Commonwealth" of Independent States. On 21 December, 1991, a gathering of representatives from eleven of the former republics met briefly at Alma-Ata to confirm this. They agreed that the formal end of the Union would come on the last day of the year. Almost immediately, Mr Gorbachev resigned. It was the climax of one of the most startling and important changes of modern history. Of what lay ahead, no one could be sure – except that it would be a period of danger, difficulty and, for many former Soviet citizens, misery.

CHINA

IN OTHER COUNTRIES, politicians were rarely tempted to express more than caution over the turn events had taken. There was too much uncertainty ahead. As for the USSR's former friends, they were silent. A few of them had deplored the turn of events earlier in the year so much that they had expressed approval or encouragement for the failed coup of August. Understandably, Libya and the PLO did so, since any return to anything like Cold War groupings was bound to arouse their hopes of renewed possibilities of manoeuvre in an international arena newly constricted first by détente between the USA and USSR and then by the growing power-lessness of the latter. Events must have been followed with special interest in China. Her rulers had their own reasons for uneasiness about the direction in which events across their longest land frontier appeared to be going after the collapse of Communism in Eastern Europe. At the end of 1991, they were now the rulers of the only multinational empire still intact. This was so although China had been engaged for most of the 1980s in a continuing process of controlled modernization, based on substantial liberal-ization (at least in the eyes of old-fashioned Communists) of the economy. This did not imply any weakening of the will to power of the régime. China's rulers remained firmly in control and intended to do so. They were helped by the persistence of the old Chinese social disciplines, by the relief felt by millions that the Cultural Revolution had been left behind, and by the policy (contrary to that of Marxism as still expounded in Moscow until 1980) that economic rewards should flow through the system to the peasant. This built up rural purchasing power, and made for contentment in the countryside. There was a major swing of power away from the rural communes, which in many places practically ceased to be relevant, and by 1985 the family farm was back as the dominant form of rural production over much of China. At the same time, it was apparent to many Chinese that China enjoyed respect and status abroad; one striking, if paradoxical, sign was an official state visit by Queen Elizabeth II in 1985.

GROWING PRESSURE FOR DEMOCRATIC REFORM

A few years after Queen Elizabeth's visit, nevertheless, China was clearly experiencing major difficulties. Foreign debt had shot up. Inflation was running at an annual rate of about 30 per cent by the end of the decade. There was anger over evidence of corruption, and divisions in the leadership (some

following upon the deaths and illness among the gerontocrats who dominated the Party) were widely known to exist. Those believing that a reassertion of political control was needed began to gain ground, and there were signs that they were manoeuvring to win over Deng Xiaoping. Yet Western observers and perhaps some Chinese had been led by the policy of economic liberalization to take unrealistic and over-optimistic views about the possibility of political relaxation. The exciting changes in Eastern Europe stimulated further hopes of this. But the illusions suddenly crumbled.

In the early months of 1989, China's city-dwellers were feeling the pressures both of the acute inflation and of an austerity programme which had been imposed to deal with it. This was the background to a new wave of student demands. Encouraged by the presence of sympathizers with liberalization in the governing oligarchy, they demanded that the Party and government should open a dialogue with a newly formed and unofficial Student Union about corruption and reform. Posters and rallies began to champion calls for greater "democracy". The régime's leadership was alarmed, refusing to recognize the union which, it was feared, might be the harbinger of a new Red Guards movement. There were demonstrations in many cities and as the seventieth anniversary of the May 4th Movement approached the student activists invoked its memory so as to give a broad patriotic colour to their campaign. They were not able to arouse much support in the countryside, or in the southern cities, but, encouraged by the obviously sympathetic attitude of the general secretary of the CCP, Zhao Ziyang, began a mass hunger strike. It won widespread popular sympathy and support in Peking. It started only shortly before Mr Gorbachev arrived in the capital; his state visit, instead of providing further

King Juan Carlos and Queen Sofia of Spain are shown on a visit to China. The Chinese government's attempts at liberalization in the 1980s were accompanied by several official visits from Western heads of state, with the aim of establishing trade relations. China needed foreign capital to accelerate its development; the rest of the world wanted access to the Chinese market of 1,200 million potential new consumers.

A lone Chinese man faces death as he tries in vain to block the path of a tank in Tiananmen Square on 5 June, 1989. More than 100 student protesters died when the army destroyed their encampment, prompting the international community to impose sanctions on China.

reassuring evidence of China's international standing, only served to remind people of what was going on in the USSR as a result of policies of liberalization. This cut both ways, encouraging the would-be reformers and frightening the conservatives. By this time the most senior members of the government, including Deng Xiaoping, seem to have been thoroughly alarmed. Widespread disorder might be in the offing; they believed China faced a major crisis. Some feared a new Cultural Revolution if things got out of control (and Deng Xiaoping's own son, they could have remarked, was still a cripple as a result of the injuries inflicted on him by Red Guards). On 20 May martial law was declared.

TIANANMEN SQUARE

There were signs for a moment that the government might not be able to impose its will, but the army's reliability was soon assured. The repression which followed was ruthless. The student leaders had moved the focus of their efforts to an encampment in Peking in Tiananmen Square, where, forty years before, Mao had proclaimed the foundation of the People's Republic. From one of the gates of the old Forbidden City a huge portrait of him looked down on the symbol of the protesters: a plaster figure of a "Goddess of Democracy", deliberately evocative of New York's Statue of Liberty. On 2 June the first military units entered the suburbs of Peking on their way to the square. There was resistance with extemporized weapons and barricades. They forced their way through. On 4 June the students and a few sympathizers were overcome by rifle-fire, tear-gas, and a brutal crushing of the encampment under the treads of tanks which swept into the square. Killing went on for some days, mass arrests followed (perhaps as many as ten thousand in all). Much of what happened took place before the eyes of the world, thanks to the presence of film-crews in Peking which had for days familiarized television audiences with the demonstrators' encampment. Foreign disapproval was almost universal.

THE FUTURE FOR CHINA

As so often in China, it is hard to know what had really happened during the Tiananmen Square crisis. Obviously the country's rulers felt they faced a grave threat. It is probable, too, that they acted in a way deplored and opposed by many of their fellow-Chinese. Yet the rural masses did not sympathize with the protesters; rather, they were against them. Changes in the ruling hierarchy and vigorous attempts to impose political orthodoxy followed. Economic liberalization was reined in. Neo-Marxist slogans were heard again. China, it was clear, was not going to go the way of Eastern Europe or the USSR. But where was she going? Perhaps the safest con-clusion to be drawn at this stage is that she was once again moving to her own rhythms and stimulants, not at once to be interpreted in categories drawn from the Western world, for all the rhetoric of régime and protesters alike. The students in Tiananmen Square met the tanks not only rallied around the statue which was their icon of liberty, but with another gesture that showed what they owed to another non-Chinese and Western inspira-tion: they sang the Internationale. That may suggest both the complexity (and even the incoherence) of the opposition movement and its alienation from much that was still influ-ential in China. As recently as 1987, a poll had reported that even among urban Chinese, the moral defect which was most strongly deplored was that of "filial disobedience". Transformed though so much of the world already was, China after Tiananmen Square still baffled observers and futurologists by her seemingly massive immunity to currents outside her borders. One of the traditional roles of her governments has always been to act as the guardian of Chinese values. If, anywhere, modernization might turn out in the end not to mean "westernization", it could be in China.

During the night of 30 May, 1989, the student protesters encamped in Tiananmen Square erected this "Goddess of Democracy" plaster statue atop the Revolutionary History Museum. It faced a portrait of Mao over the gate to the old Forbidden City.

6 EPILOGUE: IN THE LIGHT OF HISTORY

HISTORY CANNOT HAVE AN END unless we extinguish the human race; if we do not, someone will always be there to think about its past, and about his or her forerunners. History is unrolling (at a remarkably brisk pace, too) as this is being written and will go on doing so, so far as we can guess. A history of the world cannot pull up at a clean chronological boundary, nor be pinned down at a single date as a neat pattern of "significant" topics and events. The flow of actuality will in due course be plotted, studied and analysed by historians, and they will make choices and draw distinctions which make sense of it. The historically significant is always what one age thinks worth noting about another. The events of our age will acquire new meanings when people in the future start to wonder about what has made their world.

CHANGING PERSPECTIVES

Today's judgments about what is important may look eccentric even in a few months if changes come as quickly as they have been coming in the last few years. More than any of their colleagues, historians of the recent past face the old problem of perspective – a good image, which we too easily take for granted, forgetting its pictorial and visual origins. It means getting things in the right relationships to one another.

World population grows at an ever-increasing rate. Even the well-off are affected by overcrowding, as a Hong Kong beach in summer illustrates.

Road crews work to repair a broken levee near Modesto, California, after a flood in 1997. Many people blame global warming for the unusually extreme weather conditions that have struck many parts of the world in recent years. Although this is difficult to prove, we do know that the average temperature of the earth has increased by around 0.5°C since 1900 and is still rising. This is likely to result in a rise in sea-levels that will cause flooding along some of the most densely populated coastlines in the world.

In the aftermath of the huge political transformations of the last decade we all know only too well that events can alter perspective with startling rapidity. Other changes, less immediately observable, are going on, too, and may be even more fundamental. If, as some say, the startling figure of a total world population of five thousand million was probably passed on the first Monday in July 1986, and that of six thousand million by the year 2000, what are the implications of that? What can be said about the degree of damage already done to the ozone layer by the enormous increase in the burning of fossil fuels since 1945? Faced with such changes and the difficulty of assessing them, it will be best not to try to do too much, and to be content with having a last word at all. Soon, no doubt, the world will have changed still more and new surprises will make even the last few years look very different.

THE HISTORIAN'S ROLE

At the very least, prophecy must be avoided; it is not the historian's business, even if disguised as extrapolation. It may, admittedly, serve as a pedagogic or rhetorical device. It can sharpen awareness and clarify possibilities with hypothetical projections. It can sometimes demonstrate trends which cannot continue (if the world's scientists, for example, had gone on increasing in number at the rate of the two centuries down to the 1960s, the population of the world would before long consist of nothing but scientists).

Soldiers join the celebrations following the declaration of Slovenia's independence from Yugoslavia in 1991. Because of its relatively homogeneous ethnic make-up, Slovenia avoided most of the horror and violence that nationalist and ethnic disputes were already stirring up in the other regions of the former Yugoslavia.

Guesses, too, are legitimate if they throw light on the scale of present facts. Perhaps fossil fuels will go the way that the larger prehistoric mammals went at the hands of human hunters – or perhaps they will not. Thinking about the question, though, throws some light on the way the oil crisis of the 1970s, working through the blind forces of the market expressed in costs, awoke more prudent attitudes among some of the biggest consumers. But it remains vital always to recall that the historian's subject-matter is the past. It is all he or she has to talk about. When it is the recent past, what historians can try to do is to see consistency or inconsistency, continuity or discontinuity with what has gone before. Here we are back with the difficulties posed by the mass of facts which crowd in on us. The very confusion they present suggests a much more revolutionary period than any earlier one and all that has been said so far about the continuing acceleration of change confirms this. This does not, on the other hand, imply that these more violent and sweeping changes are not consistent with what has gone before, and so do not emerge from the past in a way which is explicable and for the most part understandable.

CONTINUED NATIONAL CONFLICT

I have argued in these pages that if there is any general trend at all in history, it is twofold, towards a growing unity of human experience and a growing human capacity to control the environment. Let us start there. It can be argued, for instance, that the expression "one world" is now little more than a cant term. In so far as the people who first used it hoped to ease the way to common political action, too, it seems exploded. There is just too much conflict and quarrelling about. Since 1931 there has hardly ever been more than a few weeks at a time when human beings were not fighting one another somewhere in the world. Moreover, political divisions, even when they do not break out in overt violence, can none the less be expensive and dangerous, as the Cold War showed only too well. Although there emerged from victory in 1945 an international institution called the United Nations and although it has shown some potential for collective action, it is based, ironically, on the theory that the whole surface of the globe is divided into territories belonging to sovereign states; there are now nearly two hundred of them and a strong likelihood that their number will increase. The civil war which raged until 1995 in the former Yugoslavia was, precisely, about this very issue in the eyes of many of the participants. None of this can be denied and much, much more could be said along the same lines.

Yet it does not quite meet the thesis already set out. The point could be made by thinking about a more remote period. The world of Islam during the European Middle Ages was the scene of constant strife between different Islamic rulers. Yet Islam had, none the less, a cultural unity, though not one which was complete, let alone homogeneous. All over the Islamic world, institutions and behaviour expressed this in uniformities and similarities which were not observable between other civilizations or cultures, and the societies over which they exercised their sway. That is still to a considerable extent true. One argument of this book, though, is that, for all the conflicts of the modern world, they often more and more resemble – though still far from completely – civil wars between contestants sharing a common background. A creeping unity has seized humankind. Conflicts of civilization and clashes of culture are rarer than in the past. At this level, though, the argument can hardly be put without it being overstated. More humdrum matters may make the point more exactly.

COMMON EXPERIENCE

Curiously enough, global unity is most obvious at the level of personal experience, though this is usually the level at which human beings feel most acutely the distinctions between them. In the days when the inhabitants of neighbouring villages all over the world spoke significantly different dialects even if they shared a common language, when in the whole of their lives most of them would only exceptionally travel ten miles from their homes, when even their clothes and tools might provide in their shape and workmanship evidence of big differences of technology, style and custom, then human experience was in important ways much more differentiated than it is now. The great physical, racial and linguistic divisions of the past were in their day much less easy to overcome than are their equivalents today, thanks to improved communication, mass education, mass production of commonly required artifacts, and so on. The results are obvious to a traveller in any part of the modern world. Though we can still see exotic or unfamiliar clothes in some countries, more people over most of the globe now dress alike than ever

A tourist in the Philippines photographs people in traditional dress. In many regions tourism has brought mixed blessings. Although it can often destroy traditional ways of life, it can also help to sustain village communities, along with some aspects of local cultural heritage.

These children, who live with their parents under railway platforms and near tracks in Calcutta, are pictured waiting for a train to pass. At least two railway dwellers are killed by trains every day. Similarly shocking scenes of overcrowding and poverty – of which children are often the greatest victims – can be found in cities all around the world.

before. Only rural districts or consciously nationalist régimes now cling to traditional local costume instead of the near universal shirt-and-trousers of males, for example. Kilts, kaftans, kimonos are becoming tourist souvenirs, or the carefully preserved relics of a sentimentalized past; less picturesque traditional clothing, meanwhile, is more and more the sign of poverty and backwardness. The efforts of a few self-consciously conservative and nationalist régimes only bear this out. When Rousseau encouraged the eighteenth-century Poles to national regeneration, he urged them to guard zealously their national

dress, pastimes and amusements and to reject foreign fashion. There are still régimes which are his disciples today. Uganda legislated against the mini-skirt and the Iranian revolutionaries put women back into the chador, because the common experience pouring in from the world outside was felt to be corrosive of tradition. With exactly opposite motives, though, Atatürk forbade Turks to wear the fez and Peter the Great dressed his courtiers in Western European clothes, in order to destroy tradition. More was involved than fashion. What was at stake for them was orientation towards a new range of experience, not simply taste or fashion. They had grasped the importance of symbolic immersion in what they saw as a common, advancing, progressive culture.

SHARED EXPERIENCE

The wider basis of shared experience now available to many human beings is rarely a matter of such conscious commitment to the world culture of our day. If they live in modernizing societies, they are increasingly liberated from differences of climate by electricity, air-conditioning and medicine. All over the world millions of them live in cities with similar street lighting and traffic signals, policemen on point duty, banks and bus stops. In the shops there is a growing likelihood that the same goods will be available as in other countries; toothpaste (though only invented a short time ago) can be bought worldwide. Workers who do not understand one another's languages can service the same machines and derive the same or very similar advantages and disadvantages from their use. Everywhere in the world the motor car has imposed in greater or lesser degree the same demands on urban living and threatens it with similarly intolerable strains and stresses.

The impact of cinema

When Frenchmen Auguste and Louis Lumière projected their first film, *Workers Leaving the Lumière Factory*, in 1895, the event marked the birth of what was to become a new form of artistic expression, mass communication, education and popular entertainment. The cinema, now a massive industry, has been enormously influential throughout the 20th century.

Even in the early days of silent films, film-makers were already faced with the dual demands of artistic or testimonial quality on the one hand and commercial interests on the other. Directors such as Georges Méliès (1861–1938) in France, D.W. Griffith (1875–1948), Erich von Stroheim (1886–1957) and Charles Chaplin (1889–1977) in the US, F.W. Murnau (1888–1932) and Fritz Lang (1890–1976) in Germany and Sergei Eisenstein (1898–1948) in Russia laid down the artistic foundations for cinema. At the same time, Hollywood began to realize that the cinema was going to be big business and money became the objective of studios setting up as film factories. Cecil B. De Mille's 1927 biblical epic *The King of Kings* sold 800,000 seats.

This commercial–artistic polarity remained evident in the era of talking films – still mainly in black and white until 1945, although a Technicolor feature was made as early as 1935 by Walt Disney (1901–1966). Directors who continued to extend the frontiers of film art included the Frenchmen René Clair (1898–1981) and Jean Renoir (1894–1979), and the American Orson Welles (1915–1985). Others such as the German Ernst Lubitsch (1892–1947) and the Englishman Alfred Hitchcock (1899–1980) were able to impose a strongly personal style even while working within the big studios whose box-office driven productions pushed Hollywood's takings up to $1,700 million by 1946.

The political themes of early Soviet cinema, the Nazi propaganda films of Joseph Goebbels, and the more positive social messages of post-war Italian neo-realism already showed the power of film to influence human attitudes and behaviour. New Wave French directors of the 1960s displayed increasing ease in using the camera to "write" films that seemed to dissolve the boundaries between reality and imagination. Cinema's more recent marriage with television and video has vastly increased the ability of film-makers to project lifestyles, dreams or aspirations worldwide. For better or worse – and film continues to range between art and mindless entertainment – no other medium has contributed so much to the advance of a global culture in the 20th century.

Charlie Chaplin is pictured on the set of his film The Great Dictator (1940), *in which he mocked Adolf Hitler.*

A policeman in Sudan attempts to control a crowd of starving people struggling to get access to grain provided by foreign aid agencies in 1985. Sudan is now considered a "Fourth World" country: one where food and water shortages and wars regularly cause famine.

Country districts still escape many of these blessings, but the shared experience is clearly to be seen in the cities – and in some of the world's greatest cities it is for millions an experience of uniform squalor, economic precariousness and comparative deprivation. Cairo, Calcutta and Rio can offer similar spectacles of misery, for all the important differences between Muslim, Hindu and Christian origins.

The point can be made by an effort of historical imagination. A traveller who went from imperial Rome to the Han capital of Loyang would have wondered at everything he saw; not only would clothes have been cut differently and made of different materials, but food would have been different, the animals in the streets would have been of different breeds, the weapons of the soldiers and their armour would have been shaped differently. Even wheelbarrows would have had a different design. Modern American or European travellers find much less to surprise them. China is perhaps still one of the cultures most resistant to external trends, but even if Chinese cuisine retains its distinctiveness, a Chinese airliner now looks like any other. Yet not so long ago, when junks were the only ocean-going Chinese shipping, they did not at all look like contemporary European cogs or caravels.

THE STARK DIFFERENCES BETWEEN RICH AND POOR

It can be said that shared experience is peripheral to the lives of the peasant masses who still live in villages and struggle to get a living from the soil, often with traditional tools and ideas. It is also true that the all-too-visible difference between life in rich and poor countries far transcends any difference which existed in the past. A thousand years ago all societies were by modern standards poor and consequently closer to one another in their experience than they are today. The difficulty of winning one's daily bread and the fragility of a person's life before the mysterious, implacable forces which cut him or her down like grass were things everyone had in common, whatever language they spoke or creed they followed. Now, a large minority of us live in countries with an average per capita annual income of over $3,000, and millions of others in countries where the corresponding figure is less than one-tenth of this sum. There are even colossal distinctions among the poor; people have begun to talk of a "Fourth World" as countries of the Third World which enjoy natural resources in great demand have begun to show a potential for self-sustained development virtually inconceivable to the truly poor.

This is all part of the complex reality of our world, and is not to be overlooked, yet the importance of such contrasts can be exaggerated. They are, in the first place, the product of a relatively recent and brief historical era; we should no more assume they will endure for centuries than we may assume they will easily or swiftly disappear. Perhaps they will dwindle in a world which becomes still more homogenized. The leading classes and élites even in the poorest countries almost always look to some version of modernization as a way out of their troubles. They look, that is to say, to the West. Their societies, wherever they display vitality and an urge to change, thus provide new confirmation of the pervasive influence of the civilization which has proved so triumphant elsewhere.

EUROPE AS A WORLD-SHAPER

It is not a counter-argument to say that modernization is only a matter of technology and that more fundamental matters of belief,

The Declaration of Human Rights

"Article 10: Everyone is entitled in full equality to a fair and public hearing by an independent and impartial tribunal, in the determination of his rights and obligations and of any criminal charges against him.

"Article 11: (1) Everyone charged with a penal offence has the right to be presumed innocent until proved guilty according to law in a public trial at which he has had all the guarantees necessary for his defence. (2) No one shall be held guilty of any penal offence on account of any act or omission which did not constitute a penal offence, under national or international law, at the time when it was committed. Nor shall a heavier penalty be imposed than the one that was applicable at the time the penal offence was committed."

An extract from the *Universal Declaration of Human Rights*, published in 1948.

institutions and attitudes are the real determinants of social behaviour. Not only does that sidestep questions about the way material experience shapes culture; it is easy also to point to the evidence that ideas and institutions, too, as well as material artifacts and techniques, have become more generally spread among human beings. Our world has been slow to give much practical respect to such documents as the United Nations Declaration of Human Rights, but the interest shown in drawing them up and signing them has symptomatically been intense. Although many of the signatories have little intention of respecting them, a "decent regard for the opinion of mankind" – to borrow a historic phrase – compels them to pay lip-service to certain principles. Such principles usually turn out to be derived from the European tradition of civilization (as, indeed, the widespread acceptance of the notion of a

This image of visitors to Luna Park, a Western-style fairground in Tehran, in 1994, demonstrates that certain global icons cross religious and cultural divides.

"Declaration of Rights" suggests) and this is only a recent example of the tendency of the last three centuries during which that civilization has extended its influence around the whole world. We sometimes now call that influence "Western", rather than European, but its ultimate origin and the heartland of the civilization which created it is still Europe, even if North America now so importantly shapes it. The great age of Western political domination has now passed, but the reasonable grounds for talking of the first world civilization have already been set out. It is not culturally arrogant to remark that Aztec and Inca civilizations could not stand up to the Spanish, and that Hindu and Chinese civilizations were somewhat more successful against later "Franks". Such things are true or untrue: they are neither admirable nor repugnant. Whether we regard the European tradition as greedy, oppressive, brutal and exploitative, or as objectively improving, beneficent and humane, is neither here nor there. It was either the master-source of the modern world or it was not and that is all our concern here.

As this book has argued at what some may regard as perhaps excessive length,

European ideas and institutions have by no means everywhere displaced native tradition. That is not the point. Our world is, indeed, still shaped by many deeply different traditions. Women are not treated in the same way – whether for good or ill is irrelevant – in Islamic and Christian societies. Indians still take into account astrology in fixing the day of a wedding, while English people may find train timetables or imperfect weather which they believe to be "scientific" more relevant. Though the philosophy (or what is taken to be the philosophy) of ancient Asia may have a cult attractiveness for a minority of modern Americans, the roots of American behaviour are still to be found, if in any ideological source, in the confidence of the Enlightenment and the conviction felt by many early Puritan settlers that they were a people set apart, freemen of a city builded on a hill, or that of later emigrants that they were truly entering a New World. One could go on and on with such contrasts. Differing traditions make even the use of shared technology and ideas different. Japanese capitalism does not work in the same way as British, and any explanation must lie deep in the different histories of two similar peoples. What remains true in spite of this is that no other tradition has shown the same vigour and attractiveness in alien settings as the European: it has no competitors as a world-shaper.

THE SPREAD OF DEMOCRACY

Even the grossest manifestations of the European tradition, its material greed and rapacity, show the power of its influence. Societies once rooted in changeless acceptance of things as they are have taken up the belief that limitless improvement in material well-being is a proper goal for them. They have thus taken aboard much of the mental heritage of an expanding Europe. The very idea that willed change is possible is itself deeply subversive. Many other such European ideas have imposed a layer of assumptions and myths drawn from the experience of European liberalism on top of social institutions of great antiquity and toughness in many countries. There are republics the world round nowadays, and everyone speaks the language of democracy and the rights of man. There is an effort, too, to bring to bear the rationalizing and utilitarian approach to government and administration and to replicate elsewhere models of institutions which have been found successful in countries in the European tradition. One reason why many black people clamour vociferously against the white-dominated societies they live in is that they in fact wish to realize the ideals of human rights and dignity evolved by European civilization. Meanwhile, their black cousins in new nations wish to participate in the benefits of the rising wealth made possible by industrialization and hope to realize the values it generates even when preaching the merits of *négritude* or the timeless truths of Islam.

Very few cultures, if any, have been able altogether to resist this vigorous European tradition: even China has bowed to Marx and science. Some have resisted more successfully than others, but almost everywhere the individuality of other great civilizations has been in some measure sapped. When modernizers have sought to take some things but not others from the dominant mode, they have not found it easy to do so. It is possible, at a certain cost, to get a selective modernity, but it usually comes in a package, some of whose other contents may be unwelcome, as *sotto voce* protests about pressure to give more attention to human rights showed at the 1991 conference of British Commonwealth prime ministers.

THE ADVANCE OF FEMALE EMANCIPATION

The emancipation of women makes the point: its impact on family structure and authority, on economic life and culture, and through them upon the emotions and attitudes of individuals, would be bound to prove revolutionary in many parts of the world, even were it carried only so far as to produce the state of affairs often decried by feminists in advanced Western countries as inadequate. Few non-European countries and cultures have made any but partial concessions to the principle; in some Arabic-speaking countries girls now go to universities but they

The advance of democracy

Throughout the 20th century, the number of de facto democratic countries, with universal suffrage, multi-party politics and equality for all citizens, has generally increased. Although democracy suffered a setback in the 1930s owing to the spread of Fascism, it recovered steadily after the Second World War. Since the collapse of Communism in 1989, democratic constitutions have been adopted by many of the former members of the Eastern bloc.

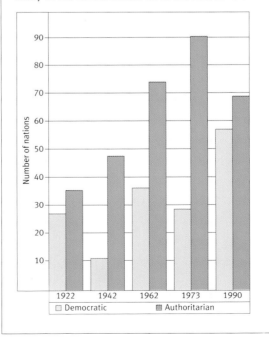

are segregated in the lecture rooms, from which they will emerge to take their places in an Islamic world where the relations of the sexes are ruled by tradition. As for uneducated women – above all the millions of peasant women of Africa and Asia – they often remain wholly untouched even by such changes. Yet they, too, may benefit directly and practically from the difference made to their lot by the arrival of modernity in the shape of pumped water or electricity in their villages, and such things have ultimately a power to transform. Not all such disparities are the result of conscious selection from the European tradition. Organic change always comes about only slowly and sometimes indirectly.

Female liberation, indeed, has taken a long time to come as far as it has done even in Western countries. Christianity had from the start a fundamental (even if at first sight barely visible) bias towards the improvement of the lot of women, because it took for granted that they, like men, had souls of infinite value in the eyes of God. On this was to be built the modern freedom of women in societies in the Christian tradition. However theologians might chip away at the idea in the interests of male prejudice they could not in the end gainsay the principle. Yet it still took some seventeen centuries to produce the first advocates of feminism and another two to arrive at the substantial legal equality of men and women in the West today. It needed, too, the reinforcement provided by industrialization, and its economically liberating effects upon women, before this could be achieved. The difference made to Western women's lives by technical change in a huge diversity of forms, from the coming of running hot water, to the perfection of detergents, synthetic fibres and prepared foods (to name only a few), has been as great or greater than that brought by the franchise.

In one of the more unusual examples of sexual equality, female conscripts are pictured on military parade in Israel, where national service is compulsory for both men and women.

SELECTIVE BORROWING

Conscious rejection of some elements in the modernization package, the sheer inertia of well-established cultural patterns and the relative accessibility of the material as opposed to the moral products of the European tradition, sufficiently explain why modernizing change still sometimes seems superficial. It is a little like Hellenization in the Near East in the centuries after Alexander. Borrowed institutions, ideas and styles often show something of the same lack of real spirit and inspiration as the borrowings of Greek ideas in the East. There is the same spread of the signs and symbols of material achievement – nowadays dams, universities, steelworks, airlines, instead of baths, theatres, temples – the same standard forms of government and administration, the same literary and artistic fashion and even the same aesthetic. English has become the lingua franca of business and intellectual life as Greek once was. Yet the results often fail to ring true; successfully transplanted to other traditions though such things seem to have been, they are somehow not the same.

THE LURE OF MATERIAL SUCCESS

The experience of civilization now so widely diffused is not unreal or a sham, but it is inevitably selective, though hardly ever in the way would-be selectors would like. This does not invalidate the claim that for the first time in human history the variety of human experience is converging instead of diverging. The most obvious sign of this is what all parts of the world have found most seductive and compelling about European culture, its promise of material success. The real triumph of European civilization came when it began to convince people in other cultures that

through it lay the road to success for themselves. Europeanization came to be synonymous with modernization. What were then seized upon were not only techniques and institutions, not merely such superficialities as clothes and hairstyles, but goals and patterns of behaviour, and these sometimes produced incongruous and unanticipated results. The ideas of progress as limitless material improvement, of the rights of individuals to assert themselves, of nationalism as the proper basis for political organization, have all produced consequences going far beyond what was expected by those who so confidently passed on to others the recipes which they believed to underlie their own

A crafts market in Luxor, Egypt, is shown. In industrialized countries, local crafts are often protected in order to preserve cultural traditions. In many developing countries, however, crafts still play a major role in the national economy, particularly in regions where tourism is important.

success. Meanwhile, the introduction of new machines, the building of railways and mines, the coming of banks and newspapers, and much, much else, transformed social life in ways no one had willed or envisaged. The process, once begun, was irreversible. Once European methods and goals were accepted (as they have been in greater or less degree, consciously or unconsciously, by élites in almost all countries), then an uncontrollable evolution had begun. Even in the most tightly controlled essays in modernization, new and unexpected needs and demands would erupt from time to time. There now looms up a new spectre – that modernization's successes may have led to the acceptance of goals which are materially and psychologically unobtainable, limitlessly expanding and unsatisfiable in principle.

HUMAN MANIPULATION OF NATURE

The revolution in the minds of human beings which has been going on with increasing vigour for a long time – the acceptance of the idea that continuous material improvement is possible – was the climax of centuries of growing success in the manipulation of the environment. Ironically, the idea took root over all the world almost at the moment when the first misgivings were beginning to be felt about it in its birthplace. They have prompted some to pessimism. To say whether pessimism or optimism about the future is justified, though, is not (it must be repeated) the historian's job. What the historian can do is say whether history has or has not been taken into account in making a judgment

In the field of transport, the general tendency is towards standard-ization, which in practice usually means westernization. High-speed trains, such as Tokyo's "bullet" train, now carry passengers and freight in many developed countries.

One of the dams for the Three Gorges hydroelectric power station is shown being built on the Yangtze River in China in the late 1990s. The power station will be the largest of its kind in the world when it is completed. Environmentalists fear that the scheme will seriously disturb the region's ecological balance and lead to the loss of a large area of wildlife habitats.

about the present or future. Substantially, it is now often urged that humanity's undoubted success in manipulating its world is now threatened by two interconnected and observable tendencies. One is that success creates new problems, and does so perhaps too rapidly for answers to be found before irreversible damage is done. Thus we face the problems of depleted natural resources, disturbance of existing ecologies, the creation of new stresses and dangers such as those involved in gathering people into great cities. The second tendency is that the achievements of science outrun our capacity to manage the power they give us. Examples are the dangers inherent in already irreversible damage to the environment, in the proliferation of nuclear weapons or the reduction in death-rate through medical advance which leads to rapid population growth, in interference with the genetic process through *in vitro* fertilization (the first "test-tube baby" was

born in 1978, in Lancashire) or genetic engineering, or in the provision of mass communications without adequate cultural preparation. If such misgivings prove justified, then the present age will indeed seem to our successors to mark a break in historical continuity. It might imply that the progressive power to control environment which marked the whole of earlier history and all known prehistory was at an end.

AN UNCONTROLLABLE EVOLUTION

Humanity's potential inability to control its environment would certainly be a prospect not to be lightly regarded, but once again we must recall how little we can say about the future. There are still no reasons to believe that the ways of discovering techniques to meet problems in the past cannot again be

Experts predict that by the middle of the 21st century, more than 80 per cent of the world's inhabitants will be living in massive, crowded mega-cities. Plans are already being made for this near future; many of the projects currently under consideration prioritize low fuel consumption. This artist's impression of a city of the future is based on plans for a "geotropolis" – an underground Tokyo.

brought to bear successfully. There are no grounds either logical or empirical for thinking that the steady accretion of control over nature which has marked all history until now will not continue. The factor that has changed, simply, is the growth in scale and acceleration. But this applies to the search for solutions as well as to the emergence of problems. We know of nothing in the nature of the problems now facing the human race which in principle renders them incapable of solution. They may be more urgent and potentially more damaging, but this is only to say that their solution may require more urgent and radical methods, more drastic political and social change, not that they are insoluble. We may have to decide to live in a different way, but we need not assume the human race will be extinguished. There is no reason to conclude that this series of tests must prove fatal to mankind when earlier ones (the onset of the ice ages, for example) did not, though they had to be faced with far

poorer resources, both mental and technological. We have plenty of evidence of human adaptability in the past. The only clear warning which does stand out is that, whatever we do, we are likely to be gravely misled about the future if we simply extrapolate present trends. We must prepare for discontinuity as well as continuity.

THE SIGNIFICANCE OF THE FIRST LUNAR LANDING

The greatest discontinuity of recent times was the successful penetration of space and the landing of men on the moon nearly thirty years ago. But besides marking a break, that achievement embodied great continuities, too. Landing on the moon was the most complete and dazzling affirmation to that date of the belief that human beings live in a universe they can manage. The instruments for doing so were once magic and prayer; they are now science and technology. But there is a continuity in the growing confidence of humans through history that they can manipulate the natural world. It cannot be said that landing on the moon is more or less of a landmark in that continuity than, say, the mastery of fire, the invention of agriculture or the discovery of nuclear power. But it is emphatically an event of that order. It can properly be compared to the great age of terrestrial discovery. The timescales are interestingly different. Something like about eighty years of exploration were required to take the Portuguese round Africa and India; there were eight between the launching of the first man into space and the arrival of men on the moon. The target set in 1961 was achieved with about eighteen months to spare. Exploration in space is safer, too. It long had no fatalities; in spite of a few spectacular accidents, in terms of deaths per passenger-

Pathfinder reaches Mars

In 1877, Giovanni Schiaparelli, an Italian astronomer, observed some lines on the surface of Mars. Later Percival Lowell, an American, studied the planet for 15 years, declaring the lines to be "irrigation channels". At that point, science fiction took over: H.G. Wells' *The War of the Worlds* was published in 1898, and an enormous number of films have been made about aliens, frequently known as "Martians".

In 1976, the Viking I and Viking II space probes landed on Mars as part of a project costing $2,300 million. Twenty years passed before another space probe landed on the surface of the red planet. On 4 July, 1997, the NASA Mars Pathfinder probe began to explore Mars. Its mission is to study the soil and rocks on Mars, as well as searching for signs of water and evidence that would support or disprove the theory that life once existed on the planet. In order to collect data, the Pathfinder probe has an exploratory vehicle called Sojourner. The size of a microwave oven, it moves at a little over 118 ft (36 m) per hour, propelled by solar power. As well as the on-board laboratory, Sojourner has a driving system oriented by laser rays, which enables it to travel over the rough Martian terrain.

A section of the spacecraft Pathfinder, with its deflated airbags, is seen shortly after its landing on Mars.

mile travelling it is still the safest form of transport known to man, while fifteenth-century seafaring was a perilous business at best. If you did not die of shipwreck there was a good chance that tropical disease, scurvy or irritated natives might take you off. Actuarially, the risk of travelling in the *Santa Maria* – or even the *Mayflower* – must have been much greater than that faced by the crew of Apollo 11.

PREDICTABLE SUCCESSES

The comparison between twentieth-century astronauts and fifteenth-century navigators

An American astronaut on a "space walk" tests a piece of safety equipment during a shuttle mission in 1994.

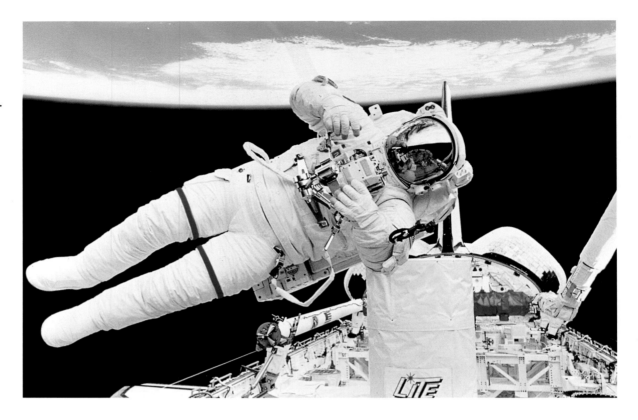

suggests another instance of continuity. The age of oceanic discovery was for a long time mainly the achievement of one people, the Portuguese. They built on a slow accumulation of knowledge. Cumulatively, the base of exploration widened as data was added, piece by piece, to what was known. Five hundred years later, Apollo was launched from a far broader base, nothing less than the whole scientific knowledge of mankind. The distance to the moon was already known; so were the conditions which would greet men arriving there, most of the hazards they might encounter, the quantities of power, supplies and the nature of the other support systems they would need to return, the stresses their bodies would undergo. In part this diminished the tremendous impact of the event. Though things might have gone wrong, there was a widespread feeling they would not. In its predictable, as in its cumulative, quality, space exploration epitomizes our science-based civilization.

Space exploration is the latest and greatest step in an increasing mastery of nature, mainly achieved in the last seven or eight millennia. That has to be set against the hundreds of thousands of years during which prehistoric technology inched forwards from the discovery that a cutting edge could be put on a stone chopper and that fire could be mastered. The weight of genetic programming and environmental pressure then still loomed much larger then than did conscious control. The dawning of consciousness that more than this was possible was the major step in the evolution of human beings after their physical structure had settled into more or less what it is today. The control and use of experience became possible with it, and then experiment and analysis. There is no need to conclude that they will not still provide humankind with a tool-kit to survive in a world which it has made so different from that of even our recent ancestors. But neither, of course, must we conclude that such a tool-kit will be found, or if found, properly and usefully employed. Pessimism is understandable – and probably temperamentally ineradicable.

NUCLEAR PROLIFERATION

One danger which does not seem quite so threatening as it did even a few years ago, certainly, is political. It no longer is solely a matter of the superpowers themselves and their ability to manage their relationships, but of the context in which the international balance must be preserved. The responsible leaders of the United States and the Soviet Union appeared even a couple of decades ago to have accepted that they could not be sure of imposing their will on the other by threat of war. They were also aware that victory in any real sense would be impossible in a full-scale nuclear war. Both began to seek agreements to limit or reduce their nuclear arsenals and both

eventually, in 1991, and thanks to major earlier political changes, announced huge reductions. These developments may well be thought reassuring. But even superpowers have to live in a world which is changing and threatened still by destabilization. Indeed, that may have become even more of a threat now that the giants no longer confront one another on an otherwise almost empty stage. It is filling up rapidly, and the bit-part players have their own lines they long to deliver. Some of them have been waiting a long time to do so and are impatient; others are frightened, and that may be more dangerous. Several countries feel they must seek to acquire nuclear weapons of their own; others emerging from a crumbling Soviet Union, find themselves de facto in possession of them. The realization that a nuclear war might mean destruction for humanity is still not shared by rulers in all countries. As long ago as 1968, Great Britain, the Soviet Union and the United States signed

In 1980 a terrorist bomb exploded at Bologna central station. From the end of the Second World War, terrorist groups have tried, through violent acts, to highlight their demands for independence, for the recovery of territories, or for their comrades in prison to be released.

a Nuclear Non-Proliferation Treaty. More than a hundred and forty other states subsequently adhered to it, but France and China (already then possessing nuclear weapons) have not done so, nor have Israel, South Africa, India (the first "non-aligned" country to detonate a nuclear device successfully, in 1974), Pakistan, Argentina and Brazil (all of whom either have effective devices, rudimentary though some of them probably are, or will have them in the near future). Grave uncertainty cloaks the nuclear future of the successor states of the USSR. In addition, Iraq and North Korea, though signatories to the 1968 treaty, are known to be trying to acquire a nuclear weapons production capacity.

CONFLICT AND COOPERATION

The proliferation of nuclear weapons must provoke sobering reflexions in a world still horribly violent, as countless deaths of men, women and children from political or quasi-political conflict have shown since 1945. And there is plenty of rubbish for new bonfires lying about. The economic ills which feed unrest in the underdeveloped world and keep it in ferment show few signs of disappearing – indeed, some would say, they have been intensified by the very globalization of economic activity which had come about through a virtually complete internationalization of capital markets and the huge surges of financial transfers which result from it, and are beyond the control of any individual government. In conditions of dangerous social tension, demagogues still inflame our problems, covert means, subversion and terrorism are still used by governments to achieve inadmissible ends, and nationalism has lost none of its power to exploit human differences. Many historical ghosts some thought long laid to rest have been released in Eastern and Central Europe

A group of Cuicurus Indians perform a traditional dance in Kari Oka, to the west of Rio de Janeiro, Brazil, where a reproduction of a traditional Amazon Indian village was set up during the "Earth Summit" of 1992. Representatives of indigenous peoples from five continents presented an Earth Charter in Rio, demanding, among other things, respect for their land, access to their countries' political systems, and self-rule.

In one of the many surprising moments of recent years, US president Bill Clinton watched as the Israeli prime minister Yitzhak Rabin and the PLO leader Yasser Arafat shook hands on the White House lawn in September 1993. After 45 years of armed conflict between their two peoples, they had just signed a preliminary peace pact, granting a period of interim self-administration to Palestinians in the Israeli-occupied territories.

in the last two or three years to harass and distract us once again.

And yet much has changed for the better. In the longest term and the perspectives of environmental damage, there is now at least recognition of problems where, even recently, none existed; there is the outline of some agreed agenda in sight. At the end of 1990 a UN conference met in Geneva with representatives of 137 nations present and concluded that global warming was a real threat to humanity. This encouraged great optimism when its preliminary labours resulted two years later in a so-called "Earth Summit", a conference on environment and development held at Rio which was said to be the largest gathering ever of heads of government. Interpretation of what was actually achieved at Rio, though, has remained very diverse; some saw it as a triumph (in that it took place at all) and others as a complete failure (in that it revealed a crippling unwillingness on the part of many individual governments to

commit themselves to specific action on such major matters as fossil fuel consumption). Yet some developed countries have, in fact already begun to show their capacity to restrict consumption of fossil fuels.

In face of a different danger, the United Nations has now at least begun to try to police international society as was hoped by some of its founders and as the League never did. In the Far East and Europe astonishing political changes have taken place which must have reduced the likelihood of war from some long-established causes.

HISTORY'S SURPRISES

Again, the historian must not prophesy (happily for him or her). If it seems disappointing to some that history can offer no grounds for unequivocal assertions one way or the other about what may be the outcome of our uncertainties, that is because they expect too much. At the end of the day, the only advantage a historian has in considering such problems is that he or she may be a little less surprised by the outcome, whatever it is, than those who have not reflected on the history behind it. Only two general truths emerge from the study of history. One is that things tend to change much more, and more quickly, than one might think. The other is that they tend to change much less, and much more slowly, than one might think. The past hangs around longer and is more difficult to keep peacefully buried, even by strenuous efforts, than we believe. That ought to be obvious enough today, after the many reminders given us in the Middle East that the wars of the Ottoman succession which began long ago in the eighteenth century in south-east Europe are still unfinished. Innovation and inertia tend to be exemplified in any specific historical situation. It was the conclusion of the first version of this book that because of this, for good or ill, we shall always find what happens somewhat surprising. More than twenty years later, there seems to be no reason to say otherwise.

The American space shuttle *Endeavour* is launched in 1993, embarking on a seven-day mission to deploy a tracking and data relay satellite. As our knowledge of space increases, proposals for space stations where groups of human beings could live for long periods of time are no longer treated as mere science-fiction fantasies.

Time chart (1949–1997)

1949
German Federal Republic and German
Democratic Republic founded

Nasser becomes
president of Egypt

1950

1952

**Fidel Castro is seen at a press
conference in January 1959. Soon
after, Cuban political parties were
repressed, elections were delayed
and Castro announced a "Marxist-
Leninist programme".**

Fidel Castro

1957
Formation of the European
Economic Community

Mao Tse-tung launches "Great
Leap Forward" in China

1958

1960

J.F. Kennedy is elected US president

**The Vietnam War began in 1964. The
high numbers of casualties on both
sides soon caused a domestic outcry in
the USA. Although President Nixon
began to withdraw troops in 1970, the
war did not end until 1973.**

US offensive in Vietnam in 1966

**In 1969, young army officers led by
Muammar Gaddafi (b.1942) staged a
military coup in Libya, overthrowing King
Idris and establishing the Libyan Arabic
Republic, an Islamic state with socialist
and nationalist leanings.**

Colonel Gaddafi

1966

1968

1965
Start of US bombardments
of North Vietnam

1967
The Arab–Israeli
Six Day War

Martin Luther King is assassinated
Soviet troops enter Prague

1973
Yom Kippur War
Military coup in Chile

Military coup in Portugal
Ethiopian army deposes Haile Selassie
and proclaims the Republic

Carter is elected US president
Mao Tse-tung dies

1974

1976

**In 1974 PLO leader Yasser
Arafat made a passionate
speech to the UN General
Assembly about the plight of
the Palestinian people.**

Yasser Arafat

1975
Franco dies and Juan Carlos
becomes king of Spain

**Mikhail Gorbachev (b.1931) became the
Soviet leader in 1985. The following
year, he announced the introduction of
policies of perestroika (restructuring)
and glasnost (openness), representing a
new liberalization of Soviet politics.**

Mikhail Gorbachev

Israel invades Lebanon

1982

1984

**Following mass demonstrations in East
Germany, the Berlin Wall was breached on
9th November, 1989, and Communist régimes
across Eastern Europe began to collapse;
Poland, Hungary, Czechoslovakia, the GDR,
Buglaria and Romania became democracies.**

The Berlin Wall is torn down

1991
The USSR is dismantled
The Gulf War

1990

1992

1989
Tiananmen Square massacre
in Peking (Beijing)

Reunification of Germany
Iraq invades Kuwait

Civil war begins
in Yugoslavia

1955
The Bandung Conference

USSR intervenes in Hungary
The Suez crisis

1954

1956

In 1962, several conferences on disarmament
were held in Geneva, attended by representatives from the United States and the USSR.
At the same time, however, multiple-head
missiles and ABMs (anti-ballistic missiles)
were being developed.

Nuclear missile

China successfully tests
its first atomic bomb

1962

1964

1961
Algeria becomes independent
The Berlin Wall is erected

In 1964, the year after US president J.F.
Kennedy was assassinated, Leonid Brezhnev
(1906–1982) became the general secretary
of the Soviet Communist Party. He is pictured
here greeting US president Richard Nixon at
arms talks in June 1973.

Brezhnev (left) with Nixon

1971
Independence of Bangladesh

1970

1972

US president Richard Nixon
visits the USSR and China

Margaret Thatcher (b.1925), British
prime minister from 1979 to 1990, was
Europe's first female prime minister. The
neo-liberal policies of the "Iron Lady"
won her ardent supporters as well as
fierce opponents.

Margaret Thatcher

1978

1980

Vietnam intervenes against the
Khmer Rouge in Cambodia

Rhodesia gains independence
and is renamed Zimbabwe

From 1958 to 1973 Pakistan
was run by military dictatorships. Benazir Bhutto (b.1953)
was the country's first elected
prime minister, from 1988 to
1990.

Benazir Bhutto

Spain and Portugal become
members of the EC
US attack on Libya

1986

1988

After 45 years of armed conflict, the
Israeli and PLO leaders signed a US-
brokered preliminary peace pact in
1993, granting a period of interim
self-administration to Palestinians in
the Israeli-occupied territories.

*Yitzhak Rabin (left), Bill Clinton
(centre) and Yasser Arafat*

1995
NATO intervenes against the
Serbs in Bosnia

1997
Great Britain returns
Hong Kong to China

1994

1996

Nelson Mandela is elected
president of South Africa

VOLUME 10 *Chapters and contents*

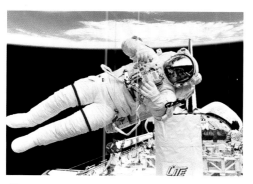

SERIES CONTENTS

INDEX

Page references to main text in roman, to box text in **bold** and to captions in *italic*.

ACKNOWLEDGMENTS

The publishers wish to thank the following for their kind permission to reproduce the illustrations in this book:

KEY
b below; c centre; t top; l left; r right
AGE: AGE Fotostock
AISA: Archivo Iconografico S.A.
CB: Corbis-Bettman
  Under Sublicence of Bertelsmann Picture Pool, Gütersloh / München 1997
FSP: Frank Spooner Pictures / Gamma
REX: Rex Features Ltd
SIPA: Sipa Press

Front Cover: NASA
3   Science Photo Library / NASA
7   CB / A. Vonlintel
8   CB / UPI
9   CB / UPI
10   CB
11   CB / UPI
12   Magnum Photos / Cornell Capa
14   David King Collection, London
15   CB / UPI
17   REX / SIPA / Dieter Ludwig
18   AISA
19   CB / UPI
20   AISA
21t   CB / AFP
21b   AGE / Steve Rubin
22   CB / UPI
23   CB / UPI
24   Magnum Photos / Fred Mayer
25   CB / UPI
26   AISA
27t   AISA
27b   AISA
28   AISA
29   AGE
30   AISA
31   CB
33   David King Collection, London
34   AISA
36   CB / UPI
37   CB
38   CB
40   CB / UPI
41t   Associated Press Ltd
41b   REX / SIPA / Olivier Jobard
42   AISA
44   CB
45   CB / UPI
46   Bettmann / UPI
47   CB / UPI
48   AISA
49   CB / UPI
50   AISA
51   Magnum Photos / Marc Riboud
52   AISA
53   AISA

55t   CB
55b   CB / UPI
56   CB / UPI
57   Camera Press Ltd
58   Magnum Photos / Ian Berry
59   CB / UPI
60   Magnum Photos / Peter Marlow
61   CB / UPI
62   REX / SIPA / Durand
63   REX
64   CB
65   CB / UPI
66   CB / UPI
68   Magnum Photos / Constantine Manos
69   CB
70   CB / UPI
71   CB / UPI
72   CB / UPI
73   CB / UPI
75   REX / SIPA
76   CB / UPI
77   CB
78   CB / UPI
79t   CB / UPI
79b   CB / UPI
80   Magnum Photos / S. Raskin
81   AGE
82   AGE
83t   CB
83b   AGE / Mark Stephenson
84   AISA
85   CB / UPI
86   CB / UPI
87   Magnum Photos / Bob Adelman
88   Zardoya / Magnum Photos / Eli Reed
89   CB / UPI
90   CB / UPI
91   Magnum Photos / Ian Berry
92   Magnum Photos / Philip Jones Griffiths
93   CB / UPI
94   Magnum Photos / Marc Riboud
95   CB / UPI
96   CB / UPI
97   Magnum Photos / Josef Koudelka
100   CB
101   Hulton Getty
102   CB
103   CB
104   FSP / Gamma
105   Zardoya / Camera Press / Peter Francis
106   FSP
107   REX / SIPA / Adenis
109   REX / SIPA / Alix
110   CB / UPI
111   Zardoya / Magnum Photos / New China Picture Company
112   AGE
113   Network Photographers / Christopher Pillitz
114   FSP
115   Zardoya / Magnum Photos / Richard Kalvar
116   Network Photographers / Roger Hutchings
117   CB / UPI
118   FSP

119   AGE
120   CB / UPI
122   CB / Reuters
123   AGE
125   REX / SIPA
126   CB / UPI
127   CB / Reuters
128   REX / SIPA / Krpan
129   REX / SIPA
130   REX / SIPA
131   CB
132   Archive Photos / Reuters / Patrick de Noirmont
133   AGE / Network Photographers
134   CB / Reuters
135   CB / Reuters
136   Zardoya / Camera Press / N. Blickov
137   REX / SIPA / Novosti
138t   CB / Reuters
138b   CB / Reuters
139   AISA
140   Magnum Photos / Josef Koudelka
141   Contifoto / Sygma / G. Dkeerle
142   Magnum Photos / Peter Marlow
143   Network Photographers / Witold Krassowski
144   FSP
145   Panos Pictures / Heidi Bradner
147   REX / SIPA / Jaques Witt
148   Magnum Photos / Leonard Freed
149   Network Photographers / Anthony Suau
150   REX / Sunday Times
152   CB / Reuters
153   CB
154   Zardoya / Camera Press
155   Archive Photos / Reuters
157   FSP / Chip Hires
158   Sally & Richard Greenhill Photo Library
159   Archive Photos / Reuters / David Ake
160   CB / Reuters
161   Sally & Richard Greenhill Photo Library
162   Archive Photos / Reuters / Kamal Kishores
163   United Artists (courtesy Kobal Collection)
164   CB
166   Magnum Photos / Jean Gaumy
168   Network Photographers / Homer Sykes
169   AGE
170   CB
171   Network / Saba / Robert Wallis
172   Zardoya / Camera Press / Yung Kwan Chi
173   Archive Photos / Reuters / NASA
174   Science Photo Library / NASA
175   CB / UPI
176   FSP / Antonio Ribeiro
177   CB / Reuters
179   Science Photo Library / NASA

MAPS AND DIAGRAMS
Maps and diagrams copyright © 1998 Debate pages 13, 99, 167
Maps and diagrams copyright © 1998 Helicon / Debate pages 16, 35, 43, 54, 67, 98, 146

TEXT CREDITS
The publishers wish to thank the following for their kind permission to reproduce the translations and copyright material in this book. Every effort has been made to trace copyright owners, but if anyone has been omitted we apologize and will, if informed, make corrections in any future edition.

p.11 extract from The North Atlantic Treaty. Reproduced by permission of the NATO Office of Information and Press from the NATO Handbook (1995 Edition).